TRADITIONAL ASTROLOGY
FOR TODAY

An Introduction

BENJAMIN DYKES

TRANSLATOR OF GUIDO BONATTI'S
BOOK OF ASTRONOMY

The Cazimi Press
Minneapolis, Minnesota
2011

Published and printed in the United States of America
by the Cazimi Press
621 5th Avenue SE #25, Minneapolis, MN 55414

© 2011 by Benjamin N. Dykes, Ph.D.

ISBN-13: 978-1-934586-22-8

ACKNOWLEDGEMENTS

I would like to thank the following friends and colleagues, in alphabetical order: Chris Brennan, Frank Clifford, Demetra George, Leisa Scheim, Robert Schmidt, and my teacher Robert Zoller. I would also like to thank the many attendees at my talks and seminars, for helping me to articulate many of the ideas presented in this book.

Also available at www.bendykes.com:

Two classic introductions to astrology, by Abu Ma'shar and al-Qabisi, are translated with commentary in this volume. *Introductions to Traditional Astrology* is an essential reference work for traditional students.

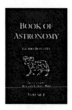

The classic medieval text by Guido Bonatti, the *Book of Astronomy* is now available in paperback reprints. This famous work is a complete guide to basic principles, horary, elections, mundane, and natal astrology.

The Search of the Heart is the first in a new horary series, and focuses on the use of victors (special significators or *almutens*) and the practice of thought-interpretation: divining thoughts and predicting outcomes before the client speaks.

The Forty Chapters is a famous and influential horary work by al-Kindi, and is the second volume of the horary series. Beginning with a general introduction to astrology, al-Kindi covers many horary topics such as war, wealth, travel, pregnancy, marriage, and more.

The first volume of the *Persian Nativities* series contains *The Book of Aristotle*, an advanced work on natal astrology and prediction by Masha'allah, and a beginners-level work by his student Abu 'Ali, *On the Judgments of Nativities*.

The second volume of *Persian Nativities* features a shorter, beginner's level work on nativities and prediction by 'Umar al-Tabari, and a much longer book on nativities by his younger follower, Abu Bakr.

The third volume of *Persian Nativities* is a translation of Abu Ma'shar's work on solar revolutions, devoted solely to the Persian annual predictive system. Learn about profections, distributions, *firdariyyat*, transits, and more!

This compilation of sixteen works by Sahl bin Bishr and Masha'allah covers all areas of traditional astrology, from basic concepts to horary, elections, natal interpretation, and mundane astrology. It is also available as two separate paperbacks.

Expand your knowledge of astrology and esoteric thought with the Logos & Light audio series: downloadable, college-level lectures and courses on CD at a fraction of the university cost! It is ideal for people with some knowledge of traditional thought but who want to enrich their understanding.

TABLE OF CONTENTS

TABLE OF FIGURES

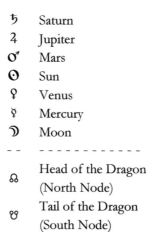

♄	Saturn
♃	Jupiter
♂	Mars
☉	Sun
♀	Venus
☿	Mercury
☽	Moon

-- - - - - - - - - - - -

| ☊ | Head of the Dragon (North Node) |
| ☋ | Tail of the Dragon (South Node) |

Figure 1: Symbols of the planets and Nodes

♈	Aries
♉	Taurus
♊	Gemini
♋	Cancer
♌	Leo
♍	Virgo
♎	Libra
♏	Scorpio
♐	Sagittarius
♑	Capricorn
♒	Aquarius
♓	Pisces

Figure 2: Symbols of the signs

INTRODUCTION: *Ye Olde Astrologie...*

If you're keen on astrology, you've probably noticed a recent revival of "traditional" astrology. Maybe you've attended a local talk on it, or downloaded a lecture, or seen a translation by me or someone else online or in a bookstore. Maybe you're intrigued and want to learn more, but aren't sure where to start. Maybe you've even been turned off by strange Arabic terms, or references to fate, or what seem to be doom-and-gloom interpretations. And yet, lots of people are being turned on to traditional approaches. You might be skeptical that something from 1,500 years ago could be relevant today. Aren't we all more evolved now, haven't we outgrown this old stuff?

This book is for you, the curious modern astrology student or practicing professional. Do you:

- Want an introduction before spending more time and money on traditional books or courses?
- Want to supplement your current practice with traditional techniques?
- Need basic objections to traditional astrology answered?
- Seek a quick guide to basic ideas, vocabulary, history, and the names and works of older astrologers?
- Need an up-to-date reference guide to the best, current books in English?

This book is designed to fulfill all of these needs.

I'm here to tell you that traditional astrology is vibrant, dynamic, and has a lot to offer: interesting predictive techniques, a vocabulary that will help you make more concrete interpretations, and a variety of spiritual and philosophical views that you may already largely agree with. I can't explain everything in this book, but I can guide you through some basic differences between traditional and modern approaches, and help you figure out where to go from here. Even if you don't become a full-fledged traditionalist, you will still improve your astrology with the concepts and techniques in this book.

I will focus on natal astrology, but just about everything I say also applies to horary, event charts, elections, and mundane astrology. In Part I, I'll outline the basic periods in traditional astrology, along with a few "need to know" astrologers. Then I'll describe some traditional outlooks on life, value theory, and counseling strategies. In Part II, I'll go further with special terms and techniques, sometimes contrasting traditional and modern, but always focusing on how you can use these ideas in a practical way. I'll conclude by answering some frequently-asked questions and challenges about traditional astrology. The Appendices and Glossary provide other valuable information and resources.

Throughout this book I want to reassure you about something very important. Many people can get the mistaken impression that following traditional practices means *abandoning* whatever else you've done in astrology—as though traditional astrology is just a series of "No's" to anything modern. Actually, there is much overlap between modern and traditional practices, and many contemporary traditionalists even use outer planets and even asteroids. Adopting traditional practices mainly involves a shift of emphasis and priority, not the rejection of everything else. Sometimes when I talk about these things with friends who practice the latest of techniques in modern astrology, it can seem at first that we have nothing in common; but after a few minutes we realize that we actually agree on a lot. But it's been so long since our community has engaged in these debates and dialogues, that at first the differences might seem too stark to be overcome. I hope to change some of that through this book.

If we had to list some basic assumptions in modern astrology, we might mention these: a belief in indeterminate free will, positive thinking, being able to create your own reality to a very high degree, and using the chart in constructive ways to show opportunities and alternatives. Actually, I don't see serious problems with some of this, provided that as astrologers we aren't simply saying "anything goes." Any view of life that says anything is possible at any moment, simply because you believe it or will it, will fail. Of course, even modern astrologers don't really go this far when looking at a chart. But we have been so out of practice in these types of discussions, that many modern people can find themselves endorsing extreme views like that because the alternatives are not well known.

Traditional thought is not so much opposed to everything modern, but requires a difference of emphasis. Let me suggest a list of assumptions and values that animate traditional astrology, divided into two groups.

(1) First are the more moral and spiritual values and concepts. I would include the following: (a) *Sympathy* for the human condition. Because we live in a complicated world we cannot fully control and understand, there is a lot

of misery whose source often some from within us. Some of this misery is reinforced by denial and wishful thinking, as natural defense mechanisms. Then, (b) the cultivation of *patience*. This kind of positive thinking means that we have to understand how our goals fit into the ebb and flow of things around us: we cannot get everything we want right away, but must rely on good timing (such as elections and opportune times predicted from the nativity). (c) Realistic *choice*, as opposed to indeterminate free will. We all have our own characters that are very difficult to change or go against, and we live in a web of events presenting certain limited and ambiguous choices—few of which are absolutely good or absolutely bad. Finally, (d) constructively *managing* who we are, as opposed to absolute self-creation and absolute spontaneity. We all have certain natural gifts and benefits, and certain drawbacks to our characters and lives, and both interpretation and prediction help us manage those things according to our understanding of conventional goods and our spiritual paths. I will discuss some of these ideas more in later chapters.

(2) Second, traditional astrology relies on rigorous and organized methods that help us train our thought and identify what is astrologically important at any point in our interpretations and predictions. I will discuss this point especially in Chapters 12 and 13.

Traditional astrology has significant contributions to make to the astrological future. In terms of philosophy and psychology, traditional astrology draws on a broader choice of value systems than many modern systems do, and makes a serious commitment to moral values and a concrete notion of human flourishing. It also provides more realistic treatments of choice and freedom, tempering modern notions of absolute personal freedom. It would also be valuable to revive the theory of temperaments which is already partially familiar to psychological astrologers, but is also connected to herbal and other holistic medicine. In terms of magic and practical spirituality, through traditional astrology we may recover Neoplatonic and other metaphysical approaches to astrology, which emphasize not simply chart reading but practical engagement with, and an active spiritual connection to, higher levels of being. These practical attitudes allow us to reach beyond our own minds and characters, and participate with the Divine Mind in the administration of the universe. I can't describe the details of all of these ideas in this short book, but as the traditional revival continues, you will be able to learn and do much more in this exciting field!

PART I: HISTORY, IDEAS, VALUES

CHAPTER 1: A HISTORY OF TRADITIONAL ASTROLOGY IN A FEW PAGES

We astrologers like to talk about the antiquity of what we do, but many people don't know much about the practices and people that actually made our history over the last 2,000 years. Don't worry, I'm not going to overwhelm you with names and dates! Appendix A directs you to books on that sort of thing. In this chapter I simply want to give you an outline of the basic periods and name some "need to know" figures in them. This will give you a general orientation to our heritage.

The way I look at it, the period of traditional astrology lasted from about the 1st Century BC in the Mediterranean, to the 17th Century in England and continental Europe, starting with works in Greek and ending in English and Latin. (There is some disagreement about exactly what dates and people define the "bookends" of this vast period.) But I should make clear that I am talking about "horoscopic" astrology here: that is, astrology that uses charts with an Ascendant (rather than omen-based astrology). This is the kind that you and I practice, with its full-blown use of planets, dignities, signs, houses, aspects, and a number of the predictive techniques you already know. I won't be discussing ancient Babylonian or pre-Hellenistic Egyptian practices (whose exact nature and history are controversial).

Hellenistic period (1st Century BC – 6th Century AD):

Our first period starts in the Greco-Roman world, particularly in Alexandria. By the time of Alexander the Great's conquest of Egypt and the Near East (even up into India) in the 330s BC, at least some horoscopic natal astrology was being practiced. But certainly by the 1st Century BC, Egyptian, Babylonian and Persian practices had been combined and enhanced to form the complex system of astrology we understand today: signs, houses, planets, rulerships, aspects, numerous predictive methods, Lots (or "Arabic Parts"), divisions of the planets into malefics and benefics, diurnal and nocturnal planets, and so on. Because Alexander's conquests more or less unified the whole region through Hellenistic culture and the Greek language, many different approaches to astrology were widely available in Greek-language books.

Really, the energy of the astrological world centered on the Egyptian city of Alexandria, with its famous library: from here we get two of the most famous ancient astrological writers, Claudius Ptolemy and Vettius Valens (though they seem not to have known each other). One of the more famous astrological books from this period claimed to be co-written by an earlier Egyptian Pharaoh (Nechepso) and a priest (Petosiris), and for many centuries it was used and quoted by astrologers. Unfortunately, it only survives in little excerpts, and was written in such a way that even ancient astrologers had some trouble understanding some of its techniques.

There is some controversy over how this complex system of astrology was developed, especially since there is little record of its details before the 1st Century BC. Was it a slow accumulation of information over millennia, or cleverly crafted by a small group of people in a short amount of time—or a combination of these? Because the ancient astrologers had books claiming to be written by legendary people like Hermes Trismegistus and others, by the 1st Century AD even they might not have known the answer. In fact, we are missing so much original material from this period, we may never know the answer in detail.

Hellenistic astrology spread throughout the Greco-Roman world, and mixed easily with the numerous mystery religions and philosophies and types of magic that were also available, such as Gnosticism, Platonism, Stoicism, and so on. (I will discuss some of this in Chapter 2). It was considered a respectable scientific practice, and in fact formed one half of astronomical science: whereas mathematics tells us how the heavens move, astrology tells us what the movements mean. And this is a good place to dispel one important myth: that the use of whole-sign houses and aspects in the Hellenistic period (see Chapters 9-10) was a result of Greek mathematics being very uncertain and imprecise. Nothing could be further from the truth. In fact, medieval and Renaissance changes to ephemerides and astronomical theory were really only refinements of earlier books like Ptolemy's great *Almagest*. Ptolemy's astronomy lasted so long precisely because it was so sophisticated and gave such accurate results.

From the 3rd to 7th Centuries AD, we get something of a two-way split in Hellenistic astrology. In the Roman Empire (now centered in Constantinople), astrology's creative period seems to have petered out. But this decline overlapped with a great excitement in the Sassanid Persian Empire, whose rulers and scholars encouraged the translation of Greek astrology books into Pahlavi (an old Persian language), in addition to making their own contributions. We'll turn to the Persians and Arabs next.

People you need to know:

- **Dorotheus of Sidon** (1st Century AD). Wrote a book on nativities and elections in poetic form, usually called the *Carmen Astrologicum* ("Astrological Poem"). Dorotheus provided absolutely essential source material for medieval Persian and Arabic writers.
- **Vettius Valens** (120 AD – ca. 175 AD). Living in Alexandria, Valens wrote the *Anthology*, a nine-part book centering on nativities, with numerous predictive techniques not found elsewhere.
- **Claudius Ptolemy** (2nd Century AD). A prolific scientific writer in Alexandria, he is best known for his *Almagest* (on astronomical theory and equations) and his *Tetrabiblos* (on natal and mundane astrology). Ptolemy's astrology was not very popular until the Latin Middle Ages, when he was revered for his natal material. Ptolemy himself claimed that he was simplifying and streamlining the tradition of his day, so much material found elsewhere in Hellenistic astrology is missing from his book (for example, of the Lots, he uses only the Lot of Fortune).
- **Antiochus of Athens** (perhaps 2nd Century AD). His identity is somewhat disputed, but he is important for a set of definitions of astrological configurations (like besieging, application, and so on) rarely found elsewhere in this period.
- **Firmicus Maternus** (4th Century AD). A lawyer and scholar, he wrote his large *Mathesis* as a work on natal astrology in eight books. He is notable for writing in Latin, which was unusual in the ancient period. Firmicus also preserves much material that is otherwise rare or lost.
- **Rhetorius of Egypt** (6th or 7th Century). Rhetorius wrote an important natal compendium drawing on Antiochus and many other authors. He was very important for later Persian and Arabic astrologers such as Māshā'allāh.

The Sassanian Persians (226 AD – 651 AD)

The Sassanian Persian empire began in 226 AD, and flourished until it was conquered by Muslim armies in 651. Unfortunately, we do not have a lot of material in Pahlavi, because during the invasions much Persian (or Pahlavi) astrological literature was destroyed. Still, chief texts survived until at least the late 700s: Pahlavi and Greek editions of the *Anthology* of Valens, the *Carmen* of Dorotheus, and others. Other works in Greek and Pahlavi appeared later under different forms in Arabic, deriving from places such as Harran, which was a center of astrology, Hermetic magic and philosophy, and star worship.

We don't know much about the Persian astrologers. But three names do stand out. Buzurjmihr was perhaps a 6th Century minister to the Sassanian ruler Khusrau I, though he may really have been a Burjmihr (of the same period), who introduced chess into Iran from India. Zaradusht ("Zoroaster") lived sometime before 600 AD, and wrote a *Book of Nativities* (along with several others) in Old Persian, based on Greek material. This work on nativities is the oldest Arabic translation of a Pahlavi astrological work we have, although it is still unpublished and untranslated. Finally, there is the curious figure of Zādānfarrūkh al-Andarzaghar, whose dates are unknown but whose influence was great. He seems to have been responsible for passing on the majority of the Sassanian annual predictive system.[1] Three charts in 'Umar al-Tabarī's *Three Books of Nativities* can be dated to between 614 and 642 (near the end of the Sassanian period): since these charts illustrate the annual techniques, it is very tempting to suppose that al-Andarzaghar flourished in these last decades of the Sassanian empire.

The Arabic Period (ca. 750 AD – ca. 950 AD)

The way I look at it, medieval astrology "officially" begins around 750 AD, with the founding of the Muslim 'Abbasid dynasty in Harran. Caliph al-Mansūr (r. 754-775) took advantage of Persian astrological expertise by hiring several Persians and one Indian to draw up an election chart for the founding of Baghdad (762 AD). Just as al-Mansūr hired Persians to do his

---

[1] Much of this system is described in the *Book of Aristotle* Book IV, and Abū Ma'shar's *On the Revolutions of Nativities*, both recently translated and published by me in my *Persian Nativities* (see Appendix A).

astrology, he and his circle supported research projects in all sciences, hiring translators and scholars from the places they conquered. Thus it was in the mid-to-late 700s that key Persian figures began writing and translating into Arabic for the first time.

Some very important developments in astrology took place during the Persian and Arabic periods. First of all, this era contains our most explicit and developed discussions of two sides to horary astrology: the interpretation of thoughts, and answering questions proper. It seems that in Hellenistic astrology, there was a lot of overlap between divining a client's thoughts, answering questions, and casting electional charts. But by this period, the approaches were distinct and were dealt with in separate books. For example, astrologers applied different methods for divining a client's thoughts (and sometimes responding to issues simply on that basis) and answering explicit horary questions provided by the client.

A second contribution was the use of new mundane techniques. In Hellenistic works, there is very little on mundane astrology that goes beyond eclipses, omens, and weather prediction. But the Persians contributed a complex theory of planetary conjunctions to track periods of history, particularly centering on cycles of Saturn-Jupiter conjunctions. Early modern astrologers in the 16th-17th Centuries spent much time using these methods to understand the political tumult around them.

These contributions allowed astrologers to flesh out the four branches in horoscopic astrology:

- **Nativities**. This is natal astrology, with its annual predictive techniques.
- **Elections**. This concerns choosing times to do or avoid something, and overlaps with "event charts."
- **Questions**. Here, the astrologer casts a chart to analyze problems of the moment, posed to him at a specific hour (hence the name "horary"). There were originally two sides to this branch: the interpretation of thoughts (using special significators, including the prediction of outcomes), and answering explicit questions.
- **Mundane**. This covers politics and history, weather and natural events (including disasters), and commodity prices.

So, this period was partly about preserving Hellenistic astrology, and partly about innovating or enhancing material already present in it. The initially fruitful and exciting period of Arabic-language astrology lasted for only about two or three centuries, when the Persian writers and their work ceased to dominate. After that, the flame of astrology passed to the medieval Latins in the West.

People you need to know:

- **Māshā'allāh** (ca. 740 – ca. 815). A Persian Jew, Māshā'allāh was a widely respected and prolific astrologer, one of those hired to cast the election chart for the founding of Baghdad. Very little of his work survives in Arabic, but much of it was preserved in Latin and is now available in English.

- **'Umar al-Tabarī** (d. ca. 815). 'Umar was another Persian on the Baghdad team, and was especially known for his horary work, as well as a handy little book on nativities.

- **Sahl bin Bishr** (early 9th Century). Another Persian Jew, Sahl worked for years in the Far East as a military and political advisor. He was familiar with his predecessors' works, and wrote five very popular works on basic principles, judgments, elections, timing, and questions. Sahl's work was key for later astrologers such as Guido Bonatti (below).

- **Al-Kindī** (801 – ca. 870). The "first" ethnically Arab philosopher, al-Kindī wrote on many scientific and astrological topics. He is especially known for *The Forty Chapters* (on questions and elections) and his theory of weather prediction. He was said to be the inspiration for Abū Ma'shar's conversion to astrology.

- **Abū Ma'shar** (787 – 886). One of the most famous and authoritative astrologers, he wrote numerous influential works. The best-known in the Latin West were his *Great Introduction* to astrology, and a massive mundane treatise called *On Religions and Dynasties*, often known as *On the Great Conjunctions*.

The Medieval Latin West (ca. 1100 AD – 1400s AD)

The medieval Latin-speaking Europeans largely picked up on astrology when translators in 12th Century Spain began to work on astrological, magical, Hermetic, mathematical, and philosophical works in Arabic. One translation line comes from John of Spain (or John of Seville), who worked in Toledo. Another important line comes from a group of three translators: Hermann of Carinthia, Robert of Ketton, and Hugo of Santalla. (Incidentally, Hugo was the first to translate the *Emerald Tablet* of Hermes from Arabic into Latin—the famous "as above, so below" text that we still quote today).

It's important to know that John and these other translators had very different attitudes toward translating, which affect our astrology today. John preferred to write in simple, straightforward Latin, trying to get the Arabic down word-for-word. His Latin is even easy for a beginning student to read. But Hugo and the others disliked like the flow of Arabic, and wanted to write in more stylized (and therefore complicated) Latin. Consequently, John's translations grew more popular and his vocabulary was adopted by most astrologers, while the works of Hugo and the others were largely neglected. For example, our word "exaltation" comes directly from John's vocabulary: *exaltatio*. But Hugo used the somewhat more accurate *regnum*, "supremacy, kingdom." Think of how we might view Aries differently, if we considered it to be the place of the Sun's "supremacy" rather than his "exaltation." This neglect of Hugo and the others also meant that their translations of important Arabic authors in natal and horary astrology were never widely known, which again affected the future understanding of astrology. Recently I have begun translating works by Hugo and his circle, so that their contributions will be available to the modern public (see Appendices A and B).

In the 13th Century, astrology was widely supported by military and political elites, and was commented and theorized upon by academics like St. Thomas Aquinas and his teacher, St. Albert the Great. For the next few centuries, astrology became a mainstay of university courses, especially in the faculties of medicine. A few notable figures in this period are the Italian astrologer Guido Bonatti (13th Century), an advisor to Emperor Frederick II named Michael Scot (12th-13th Centuries), and Campanus (13th Century), who devised a house system still used by some today.

People you need to know:

- **John of Spain** (fl. early 12th Century). Also known as John of Seville, he was a prolific translator of Arabic, with a very friendly Latin style. Many later astrologers used his translations as their source texts.
- **Hugo of Santalla, Hermann of Carinthia, Robert of Ketton** (fl. early to mid-12th Century). These three translators worked together in various ways around northern Spain and southern France, especially on astrological works which John of Spain did not translate. Their Latin was more stylized and difficult, which led to their translations being either neglected or criticized. I have made several of their works available in English.
- **Abraham ibn Ezra** (fl. 12th Century). A Jewish scholar and poet who lived largely in Spain, ibn Ezra wrote a number of shortish works on all areas of astrology, largely drawing on Arabic-language predecessors.
- **Guido Bonatti** (13th Century). This Italian astrologer was renowned in his times, especially as an astrological military advisor. His massive *Book of Astronomy* was an encyclopediac work based on Arabic, Greek and Latin predecessors, and became a medieval standard.

Renaissance and Early Modern Astrology (1400s AD – 1600s AD)

This period has several important features. In addition to continuing older practices, Renaissance and early modern[2] astrologers also had to confront the popularity of astro-psychological magic and therapy, an attitude of reform (especially against techniques thought to be inventions of Arabs or as not being "natural"), and new scientific vocabulary and outlooks.

For one thing, Marsilio Ficino (15th Century) published works of Plato and Hermetic writings, and developed a practice of astrological magic, emphasizing the planets' relation to the soul: the soul does not escape astrology (as some medieval argued), and planetary gods play a role as aspects of the psyche itself. For Ficino, this kind of healing is especially needed because the embodied soul tends towards depression and psychological

---

[2] I mean this in the standard historical sense of the period during and after the Reformation, and the early scientific revolution.

sickness. This attitude took up the Platonic and magical outlooks described below in Chapter 2.

Later, astrology took approximately three overlapping paths. Traditional astrologers like William Lilly had little interest in the latest theories of physics, and continued to use traditional techniques as though nothing had changed. On the other hand, there were astrological reformers. These people were bothered by bad predictions in popular almanacs and elsewhere, and worried that astrology had been polluted by various superstitions. They wanted to make a more accurate astrology that harmonized with new ideas in astronomy, and rejected what they believed were illegitimate additions from the Arabs, or anything they couldn't understand, or whatever didn't seem "real" or "natural." Unfortunately, these reformers often did not understand the true history of astrology: as I mentioned before, the Persian and Arabic writers were fully engaged with Hellenistic-era astrology, and were not very interested in adding new technical concepts. Nevertheless, the reformers felt free to reject whatever it took to streamline their practice. This reforming trend has been a central part of the re-invention of astrology in the 20th Century, including the casual dismissal of anything that seems old or strange.

Finally, astronomers and new scientific skeptics ignored astrology more and more, although they were open to the idea of planetary influences on things like weather. In part, the new materialistic and mechanistic physics was simply incompatible with older Aristotelian and Neoplatonic (and magical) outlooks. But plenty of these people still thought that perhaps modern science could improve astrology, rather than rejecting it. Nor should we think that these people were all atheists, either: plenty of them also believed in free will (which was originally a theological concept) and God, and so in a way they continued a mainstream medieval position on astrology: namely, that astrology concerns physics and natural bodies (e.g., weather, health) rather than the soul. I'll return to this in Chapter 2 below.

In terms of technical contributions and developments, this period had several:

First, there arose numerous quadrant-based house systems using intermediary cusps (e.g., Regiomontanus and Placidus) instead of the older whole-sign house system (see Chapter 9). Although many Arabic-era astrologers used quadrant houses, it is difficult to find astrological writers describing them explicitly (and many still made reference to whole-sign houses). But the use of new house systems was explicit in this later period.

Astrologers also greatly expanded the use of medical astrology and techniques for determining temperament and bodily shape. Some of these methods can be found in William Lilly's *Christian Astrology* (17th Century). In fact, medical schools commonly included astrological techniques in their curricula.

Of course, advances in mathematics led to more accurate ephemerides. Another outcome of modern mathematics and reforming attitudes was the invention of new aspects, such as the quintile (promoted by astronomer-astrologers such as Kepler).

People you need to know:

- **Regiomontanus** (1436-1476). Under this pseudonym, Johann Müller is best known for his table of houses and method of primary directions, which were widely adopted and favored by such astrologers as William Lilly and Jean-Baptiste Morin.
- **Jean-Baptiste Morin** (1583-1656). An accomplished astronomer and mathematician, his *Astrologia Gallica* ("French Astrology") was published posthumously in 1661. Morin is especially valuable for his careful and precise teaching style. He engages in many debates with other astrologers and discards various traditional techniques as being either unnatural or Arab inventions.
- **William Lilly** (1602-1681). An English astrologer and one of the earliest to write in English, Lilly was a famous master of horary astrology. His *Christian Astrology* remains a valuable classic.
- **Placidus de Tito** (1603-1668). Placidus is best known for his development of the Placidus house system, which was closely related to his method of primary directions.

The decline of astrology (17th Century AD – 18th Century AD)

There were many reasons for astrology's decline near the end of the 17th Century. But they are not quite the reasons we are usually told. The usual story is that astrology makes bad predictions and was eventually overcome by the glorious arrival of modern science (especially in astronomy and the disciplines associated with medicine). It's easy to show that this is not true, through two simple facts. First of all, people in religious and economic circles routinely make false predictions and have disputes amongst themselves, and yet those areas are doing quite well. Second, many astrologers were scientists, and some hoped to use Newtonian physics (with its "action at a distance") to support astrology. There was no unanimity about astrology among scientists.

I would like to propose the following reasons for astrology's decline, all of which were in play at the same time.[3]

(1) Astrological vocabulary matched educated people's views of the world less and less: for example, there is no scientific or academic category that can make sense of an astrological "house" or "rulership." The symbolic nature of astrology made it hard for people to understand, and astrologers themselves were often throwing away old vocabulary in an attempt to be modern.

(2) Although astrological almanacs were very popular, they were very generic and not very useful (much like modern Sun sign columns), unlike going to a professional astrologer.

(3) Reforming astrologers were more interested in getting rid of what they considered old or "unnatural" or as an invention by Arabs, than in making their own contributions—which led to an impoverished astrology. In the meantime, they were often in competition with each other as personalities, instead of cooperatively promoting astrology as an art. This was especially true in England, where astrologers attacked each other in vicious, often political pamphlets.

(4) Modern myths of progress and enlightenment encouraged people to reject anything that seemed "old"—which included astrology.

(5) Religious people often kept insisting that astrology did not apply to the soul but only to things like weather and medicine. This general attitude would also have discouraged astrological magic and spirituality.

(6) Non-religious people (whether sympathetic to astrology or not) often tended towards materialistic and mechanistic theories of the world, which did not really match the astrological world view.

(7) Finally, there is what I'd call bad, non-astrological theologies and ideologies. Many Protestant astrologers in particular published fearmongering pamphlets trumpeting the arrival of the Antichrist. Now, although there were a few ancient views about how the world would be

---

[33] In what follows, I have relied on some of Nicholas Campion's ideas in this section (see Appendix A).

destroyed when planets came to certain positions, this was not very practical information. Astrology works with cycles, and the Persian view of mundane astrology assumed periodic upheavals that would lead to further cycles. Earlier astrologers did not really speculate about Judgment Day, nor did they assume it was close! So their astrological view of history matched the astrological notion of cycles quite well. But Reformationists and Enlightenment figures (like many moderns) believed they were entering a fundamentally new period of history, which has both secular and religious versions: in secular terms it meant that we were entering a time of ultimate light and reason, but religiously it meant we were entering a time of ultimate darkness and strife. And so, these astrologers grafted what was really a Christian view of end times onto an astrology that was never fit for that. Moreover, both of these views of entering a totally new age are basically incompatible with practical astrology: if rationalistic materialism and reason are all we need, then we don't need astrology; but if we wrongly predict the coming of the Antichrist every year, then astrologers undermine themselves. I must emphasize that these two attitudes are *assumptions* of different ideologies, they are not *proven facts*. But since astrology was more or less undermined by both, it seemed less relevant and useful.

The Traditional Revival (20th-21st Centuries)

Practical astrology was more or less reinvented and popularized around the turn of the 20th Century by people like Alan Leo, Marc Edmund Jones, and others. But here I'd like to say a few things about the revival of *traditional* astrology. In my view, there have been four broad trends.

First, in the early 20th Century, European scholars of Greek labored on an ambitious new project, which was the cataloguing and publishing of Greek astrological texts: the result was a large, multi-volume work called the *CCAG* (the "Catalogue of Astrological Codices in Greek"). These scholars were historians and philologists, not astrologers; but their publications allowed astrologers to have greater access to many older texts for the first time. One of the more important results was the publication of what are called "critical editions." A critical edition is a book that is created out of all known manuscripts and printed editions of some work, so as to form what we assume was the original (or close to the original) version. Some critical editions of Hellenistic authors that have resulted from this broad effort include the *Anthology* of Valens, the *Tetrabiblos* of Ptolemy, and the *Apotelesmatics* of Hephaistio. Later in the century, the historian David Pingree published an edition of Dorotheus's *Carmen* from the surviving Arabic, with many related Greek fragments and passages. Others created a critical Latin edition of Firmicus Maternus.

Second, astrologers were re-introduced to William Lilly through the 1985 reprinting of his *Christian Astrology*, promoted by Olivia Barclay in the UK. This not only put (late) traditional astrology back on the map, but made horary astrology a defining centerpiece of traditional practice in the modern world.

Third, the impetus from Barclay and other developments has produced number of influential teachers (many of them Barclay's own students), such as Deborah Houlding, John Frawley, Sue Ward, and Barbara Dunn. On the other hand, Robert Zoller has worked independently since the early 1980s to promote medieval natal astrology (especially the work of Bonatti). Many people working professionally as traditional astrologers today are students of these important teachers (I was a student of Zoller's).

Fourth, a number of translators have made older works available in modern languages. These include David Pingree, Charles Burnett, Robert Schmidt, James Holden, Meira Epstein, Robert Hand, and myself. The number of traditional works now available in translation has exploded in recent years. One important feature of some of these translators is that they are not simply interested in publishing texts, but in resuscitating a *traditional way of thinking* which is still just below the surface even in modern minds.

Now that we've looked at traditional astrology in terms of historical periods, let's look at some of their typical outlooks on life and what they believed the role of astrology was.

CHAPTER 2: A FEW SCHOOLS OF THOUGHT

In the last chapter, I mentioned that many traditional astrologers are trying to resuscitate something of traditional thought. Now, not all traditional people or astrologers agreed in their philosophies of life or on what astrology was all about. Here I'll outline five basic schools of thought (and I will discuss some of them further later), but please keep in mind that many people had views that overlapped different categories—not everyone fits into one neat box, either then or now.

Aristotelian-Ptolemaic. I use this name because this approach roughly draws on the physics of Aristotle as well as Ptolemy's scientific justification for astrology in his *Tetrabiblos*. According to this view, the planets *cause* things to happen, they are causal agents. For example, Mars causes Martial events because he produces excessive heat and dryness, and Martial-type events have those qualities. Therefore, astrology is a virtually a branch of physics, and is in some sense part of the natural sciences. Modern astrologers who adopt terms from physics such as waves, fields of force, and so on, or who believe that modern physical concepts can be adopted so as to justify astrology, belong in this camp. For the most part, this view also allows for human freedom and choice as we conventionally understand them (though not indeterminate freedom of the will). For instance, perhaps the planets only cause certain broad trends, but these can be overridden or managed through our power of choice. Our ability to choose wisely will depend on how the planets have caused us to have a certain temperament or attitude, so even our choices are in some sense conditioned by the causal power of the planets.

Stoic. Although not everyone who expressed this view might have identified as a Stoic, it can easily be tied to Stoic philosophy. According to this view, the universe is governed and determined—perhaps down to its finest details—by an all-permeating Cosmic Intelligence or Mind. Here, events around us are caused in all of the normal ways (through natural phenomena, choice, and so on), but it is not the planets which cause them. Instead, the Cosmic Mind has established the planets as beings or objects which *signify* things. This is akin to medicine, where symptoms are caused by natural processes, but a doctor interprets these symptoms as signs, in order to make appropriate diagnoses and prognoses. So, on this view astrology is a *science of interpretation* and is divinational, not part of the physical sciences. This school also argued that while we do have the power of choice, from a cosmic perspective everything is causally determined, even one's choices. This is the most deterministic of approaches, but astrologically there is some leeway. For instance, even if a planet signifies something, it might only signify a *type* of thing—the details of what it is, may be somewhat up for grabs. I'll address this again in Chapter 15.

Platonic. This category overlaps somewhat with other views. Plato was not really an astrologer, but his interests led in that direction, and he believed that human ethical and social life should be based to some extent on the astrological universe. The lower parts of our soul (emotions, instincts, and the body) are to a large extent governed by physical forces dictated by planetary gods, and heavenly movements that stand between us and the upper, divine world. Our power of reason, which can manage these lower forces somewhat, is not as constrained, and is suited to study and commune with the eternal realities that stand above the sphere of the planets. At its best and highest level, astrology can be a tool for enlightened people to have access to God's mind and eternal reality, because planetary motions essentially map out, in a temporal way, the eternal thoughts of God. (This is close to the Stoic view.) But astrology and its insights can also be used to help less enlightened people, who could use the organizational insights of the upper worlds to understand and manage their lives in this lower world. Plato seems to suggest that astrologers should help political authorities govern citizens justly. Also, because Plato believed in reincarnation and in the idea that certain planetary powers guide our soul, some features of his thought are close to certain modern astrological views.

Christian. This fourth view drew on previous notions as well as a new theological development of the 1st and 2nd Centuries AD: that is, the introduction of an indeterminate "free will" which is liberated from the forces of necessity on earth, and which can radically self-create and change one's direction in life. According to this school, human free will is a weak mirror image of God's radically free will. However, most people do not normally exercise their free will, even when they think they are. Most of us are mired in sin and the sensual world (as with Plato). But sometimes we get help from God in exercising free will, and in its strongest form this allows for the existence of saints: unlike normal people who are subject to the natural world (and whose lives can be largely described by astrology), saints and enlightened people cannot really be captured and described by any astrological chart, since their choices and actions derive from free will. Thus, astrology properly belongs to matters such as weather, health, and the normal actions of unsaintly people. This view is also close to a generic Gnostic view, which says that most people are ignorant of ultimate reality and are subject to malefic planetary governors—but enlightened Gnostics are morally and spiritually liberated because they have access to realms above the planets. One can see echoes of Plato here.

Magical. This view has so many sources it is hard to pin down precisely: it draws on folk magic, omens, Platonism, Hermeticism, and much more. In its "lower" form, it uses auspicious planetary times, talismans, analogous plants, gems, music, and appropriate speeches, to interact with planetary powers and create favorable worldly circumstances for the practitioner. In its "higher" forms, it may include all of these practices but to the end of becoming wise, spiritually advanced, and living a virtuous life. In the Renaissance, Marsilio Ficino argued for the use of astrological magic to re-engineer and balance the soul, so his astrological magic bore the mission of psychological and spiritual transformation through the use of astrological rituals. (It surprises me that more modern astrologers do not advocate this.) This is the more "otherworldly" of the schools, and is not really included or alluded to in standard astrological textbooks—one needs to consult grimoires and other magical texts to learn the techniques.

These are the five basic traditional approaches to astrology, and I think you can probably see a lot of echoes in modern attitudes. In closing, I'd like to describe a certain view of astrology from the Middle Ages, which is still relevant today. By the 13th Century, Christian thinkers had developed a compromise blend of radical free will and Ptolemaic-Aristotelian trends. Roughly put, it made the following claims. (1) Astrology fulfills the definition of a science, because it uses experience and reason, with deductions from axioms, rules and so on, in order to explain things. (2) Because its objects of study (namely, the planets) are among the highest and best things, it is among the highest-ranking sciences. (3) The planets are causal agents, and their influences affect combinations of form and matter on the earth. (4) Astrology is compatible with freedom, *provided that* a special place is made for the radically free will. According to this view, some of our actions and choices are causally affected by our physiology, character, and so on, and these can be understood astrologically. But free will and salvation are not subject to physical causes, and so astrology cannot do things like describe our spiritual natures. Therefore, astrology pertains to weather, the body, and other worldly events not in our direct control, and even some personality and character matters; but it does not pertain to our free will and ability to be saved.

That last part is very important, because it is still with us. In this compromise view, the more holy and blessed you are, the less astrology applies to you: for, those with the highest degree of self-determination and free will and spiritual connection, are not subject to astrological causes apart from physical things like illness and weather. But the less enlightened and less free and less spiritual you are, the more astrology applies to you. This same attitude now appears among some modern astrologers, but instead of being "blessed" or "saintly" we say we are "conscious" or "evolved." In other words, some modern astrology is essentially *a secular astrology for the unsaved*. Far from being a special modern discovery based on Jung or the Theosophists, it comes right out of medieval Catholic universities, and earlier writers as well. Based as it is on an indeterminate, radically free will, it will probably remain with us so long as people believe in that kind of free will.

CHAPTER 3: IS THE CHART OUR MIND?

One of the more important things that helped me learn traditional astrology was understanding the difference between objectivity and subjectivity in a chart. In a certain sense, traditional astrology is more objective, while modern astrology is more subjective. These terms can mean a number of different things, so let me explain a bit more where I am coming from. The main distinction is this: in modern astrology, the natal chart is usually taken as a picture *of your mind*. In traditional astrology, the chart is a picture of your place *in the whole world, only part of which is your mind*.

Let's take two examples. In much modern astrology, the second house is taken to indicate "values." Now, values are something experienced through the mind: they pertain to judgments that we make about things. But think of all the things in the chart which have personal or moral value, or are actual people and things we value: money, relatives, parents, children, pleasures, relationships, spirituality, education, honor and prestige, friends. There are also things we put negative value on: slavery and sickness, death, depression and enemies. We put positive or negative values on all of these things, and there is no way we can boil all of these down to the second house. Rather, they reflect separate people and experiences in life, and many of them are out of our general control and do not reduce to opinions in our minds: they are *objective* realities.

Likewise, take the eleventh house. Traditionally this is the house of friends and friendships—not our *attitude towards* friends, but the friends and friendship experiences themselves. We all value friendship in a general way, but how people actually experience friendships, and what their friends are like, are not confined only to their own minds. Some people have many and lasting friends with their own good personalities; others have difficult and unsteady friendships, no matter what our feelings happen to be. And so, this is a key difference between modern and traditional astrology: when interpreting a chart, we cannot assume that these things are merely in the native's[4] mind, even though the native has to think about them and make decisions about them.

When I was first learning horary astrology, I had only a modern background. I read in books that a horary chart will often reflect the good or bad feelings and expectations of the client, and this matched my general assump-

---

[4] That is, the person whose birth chart or nativity it is.

tion that the purpose of a chart is to reflect the mind. But when I cast my own horary charts, such as "Does he love me?" or "Will I get the job?" I found that I couldn't tell the difference between a yes or no answer, between a good and bad result, and my own mind. I looked at Saturn and wondered, "does this indicate my worries, or does it mean that he doesn't love me after all?"

You can see something of the same difference in natal astrology. I remember interpreting the charts of relatives, and writing down every possible delineation: Pluto square the Moon, Venus in Gemini, Uranus in the eleventh, and so on. Often, many of the delineations contradicted each other. But why? Because I thought that everything in the chart had to equally indicate what was in the personality. And so, I felt completely lost. I worried that maybe I just didn't understand astrology well enough, and that after more study I'd get it. But that didn't work, either.

The traditional approach says is that most of the things in your chart are not in your mind. They are part of your life, and you experience them, but they are not you. The seventh house is your partners and spouse, not your feelings about them; the eleventh is your friends and friendships, not your feelings about them; the second house is your personal possessions (and sometimes, allies), not your feelings about them; and so on. Instead, all of these interpretations I thought were part of my relatives' *subjective* minds, were really descriptions of *objective* affairs in their lives. True, all of the planets in your chart are part of your experience: but experiences take place when interacting with an objective world. In a natal chart then, not every planetary placement indicates the native's mind, but different planets are used for different areas of life, minimizing the apparent contradictions and clashes. So the Sun might not have anything to do with you in particular in your nativity, because the Sun is not you: if he is in the ninth, he might have something to do with travel and foreigners and spirituality, but not your inner mind and personality. Venus is not you either, but because she signifies love and relationships in a general way, she'll be relevant for your sense of romance and relationships *when doing that particular delineation*. Otherwise, by her location and rulership she might simply indicate your sister or parents, or an illness, and so on.

What this leads to is something rather traditional but really common-sensical: we can be *objective* about people's *subjective* lives. Have you ever asked for advice from a friend? We often rely on our friends to tell us whether we are doing well or are going astray: we need advice, an outside opinion. The same goes for astrology: when speaking with a client or looking at a chart, we can be honest about whether things are going well or not, and often whether someone (our friend, a client) is a victim of wishful thinking. In fact, it would be *irresponsible* to tell a friend that she can create her own reality, that there is nothing good or bad, and that every apparently negative thing is just a positive opportunity or a learning experience. It's true that we can *treat* every bad thing as a learning experience, but unless we *recognize* conventionally bad things, we cannot realistically connect with a client or give advice.

One apparently strange consequence of this is that *traditional techniques do not work unless you adopt this mindset.* When my own teacher, Robert Zoller, expressed this view, it didn't make sense to me. If a technique works, shouldn't it just work? But the fact is that if you do not treat things objectively, and especially if you treat everything intuitively or as something solely in someone's mind, you will miss all sorts of important events in people's lives, and you won't be able to describe them or people's subjective responses accurately. Now, most modern astrologers actually understand this in practice: when astrologers look at transits and directions, they look at objective events and themes in people's lives which they must confront and deal with. But much of modern astrologers' *self-conception* does not allow them to officially view these things as objective, or as things not directly in our control. This can create problems with delineation. For if we assume that the chart is a picture of our mind, then since we always carry our mind around with us, we may assume that all sorts of traditional delineations are wrong: if a traditional interpretation says that there will be difficulty with the eleventh house, you might be tempted to think that there will be problems *always and every day* with the eleventh, because it is a feature of your mind. But traditionally, this theme of the eleventh house might only be very active when we apply certain predictive techniques—because it is not a constant content in your mind. I'll deal more with this in Chapter 13.

To give you an example, I once had a client with a somewhat unusual chart. At first glance, things didn't look very good from a conventional standpoint: virtually every planet was in detriment. On the other hand, virtually every planet was also aspecting the others in a way so as to bring about reception.[5] So I told the client that it looked as though his life was full

---

[5] Reception is normally when two planets are in aspect (preferably by degree and not merely by sign), where one is in the domicile or exaltation of the other. For example, if

of events and affairs where, although he was generally successful (because of the receptions), things did not last very long or encountered a lot of changes (because of the detriments). "Yes," he said, "I have always noticed that. I work freelance and am successful in what I do, but many things in life seem only to last a short time. I've always wondered if it was a problem with *me*." From a traditional standpoint I could then advise a couple of paths: work hard to overcome this tendency toward change and disintegration, or embrace it and see it as an opportunity to do many different things and have a more varied and rich experience—but he should not consider it as a matter of his character and something that was his fault.

These ideas directly affect our chart reading, in the form of *critical distance*: the ability to question our assumptions and remove ourselves emotionally from the chart. Critical distance is related to the use of interpretation rules (see Chapter 12), but also the use of the conventional values (Chapters 4 and 5). The more we assume a subjective view of the chart, the more we invite ourselves to merge our own values and visions and associations with it: we try to merge our own mind with the mind of the chart, because everything is in the mind. This temptation invites wishful thinking, such as when there's a difficult situation in the chart but we want to give people good news, or talk about their evolutionary potential, instead of pointing out something objectively unusual or difficult.

Another example is when we look at our own chart, though this is often difficult even in the best of circumstances. When things in the chart are not merely in our own minds, we can be alert to both good and bad things, not over-valuing the good or over-fearing the bad, because both are temporary and do not have an absolute ability to affect our attempt to be happy.

The same thing happens when we look at mundane charts or event charts. It is very easy to let our own value judgments enter into understanding some political event. But what if that event does not conform to our own political values? When astrologers interpret the meaning of a mundane event, their opinions often reflect their own personal values. Traditional astrology allows us some critical distance—not just in this or that situation, but in principle for all situations.

Mars were in Virgo and he was aspected by Mercury (who rules Virgo), Mars would be received by Mercury, and some of his normal Martial qualities would be tamed and civilized.

CHAPTER 4: GOOD AND BAD:
VALUES IN TRADITIONAL ASTROLOGY

To God, all things are beautiful and good and just;
but for humans, some things are just and others unjust.
-- Heraclitus, Fr. 85

Traditional astrologers often speak about something being good or bad, or planets and their influences as being benefic or malefic. This is a turnoff for many modern people. But when we speak of goods and evils, we are dealing with important ethical and philosophical concepts: what is the nature of good and evil? Are some things only apparent goods and evils? Can normal goods and evils truly affect our ability to be happy? And how can we apply these notions in a counseling context? If we refuse to recognize these values, it will be more difficult to connect with people we are trying to help.

In this chapter, I'll talk about two broad ways of thinking about good and evil, and in the next chapter I'll show how they apply in counseling contexts: in a more conventional approach to happiness (Aristotle), and in a more "spiritual" approach (Stoicism).

1. Functional values and planetary conditions

Traditional philosophers had some common ways of identifying what made something good—and for some of them, goodness was virtually equivalent to *being* something. Here are some general qualities that a situation or dynamic or person might have to have, to be good:

Knowable
Unified or organized
Consistent
Present
Balanced

Note that these qualities don't make something *morally good*. They show whether something performs its functions *well*. Their opposites suggest functioning *poorly*: things that are obscure, disorganized, inconsistent, absent, and unbalanced. It's in this spirit that traditional texts talk about planets being in a good or bad condition, or being strong or weak. So when we look at a chart, we look to see whether planets are in a good or bad *functional* condition. This helps us know whether the people and events they indicate are consistent and smooth and helpful, or unruly, full of extremes, and so on.

The following table gives you a general idea of what these typical catego-ries mean in terms of planetary functioning. Don't worry if you don't understand all of these terms yet, I'll introduce them later.

Functionally good	Functionally bad
Configured. Being in communi-cation, able to manage and be seen.	**Aversion**. Being invisible or out of communication.
Angular or succeedent. Being prominent or strong.	**Cadent**. Being obscure or weak.
Aspected by benefics. Often, encountering balanced and growth-bearing influences.	**Aspected by malefics**. Often, encountering extremes.
Domicile. In a state of unity, competence, and control.	**Detriment**. In a state of disinte-gration and disunity.
Exaltation. Being prominent and confident.	**Fall**. Being obscure, ignored, fading away.
Free of the Sun. Able to work on its own, visible.	**Combustion**. Being over-whelmed, destroyed.
In any dignity. In a place of belonging, able to depend on its own resources.	**Peregrine**. Not-belonging, dependent on external influences.
Direct. Moving forward, con-sistent, open.	**Retrograde**. Repetition, detours, hiding motives.

Figure 3: Some Planetary conditions

The idea is that every planet is trying to do its own thing well: it's trying to rule a house, stand out and be prominent, have a sense of ownership and competence, move forward with its agenda, and so on. But if it's in a functionally bad situation, it is somehow hindered. Much of the time, functionally bad placements also result in conventionally bad events (or they prevent good events). But I'll save that for later. My point is that these planetary conditions reflect real affairs in life. In life we do count it as good when we feel competent, visible, honored, and can move forward; but we feel like life has something wrong in it when our bodies are sick, we are unknown and ignored, are weak or incompetent, insecure, and can't communicate in the way we want. These functional conditions of the planets are meant to reflect that. We should welcome this vocabulary, because it helps us understand our chart and our lives more accurately!

It's partly from these sorts of ideas that we get the notion of benefic and malefic planets. Benefic planets are those whose natures normally show patience, kindness, helpfulness, balance, growth, fun, and things that are easy. Malefic planets tend towards extremes and functionally difficult things: hindrances, pushiness, imbalance or extremes, burdens, things that are more serious, threats. Of course these characteristics are very general and abstract: a malefic planet in a good condition can perform very well, show leadership skills and authority; a benefic planet in a bad condition can be lazy, erratic, lowbrow, and so on. The point is that this vocabulary helps us link chart conditions to life conditions.

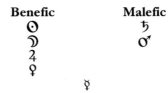

Figure 4: Benefic and malefic planets

2. Moral values and the houses

Another important use of values applies to the houses. The basic meanings of the houses typically describe what I'll call "conventional" moral values: people and experiences that have normal moral goodness or badness, and which contribute to a conventionally happy or unhappy life.

Take a look at the figure below, which gives common traditional meanings. If we start at the first house and move counter-clockwise, we see a number of things we'd normally consider morally good and beneficial: health and life, assets, family, pleasure, relationships, spirituality, reputation and career, and friends. But we also see several houses that contain conventionally "bad" or harmful things: slavery and illness, controversies or contentions, death, fear, enemies, sorrow. Several of these houses are "in aversion" to the Ascendant, which I'll talk about in Chapter 10.

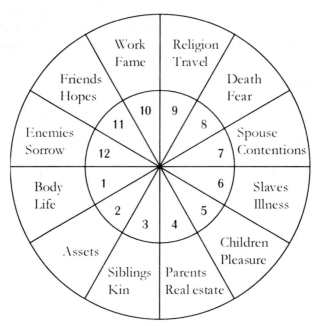

Figure 5: Basic meanings of the houses

If we look at the houses in this way, especially if we take into account planets in them and ruling them, and the planetary conditions, we are really looking at standardly-expected outcomes for a happy or unhappy life. Are there malefic planets in the fifth, or is the lord of the fifth house in a poor condition? This can reflect difficult situations with one's children—what we would normally call bad. Is there a benefic in the eleventh, in a good condition? This would indicate conventionally favorable situations for friendships: lasting friendships, friendship with good people, and so on.

This approach is well able to help us understand what is going on in people's normal experiences. We haven't applied predictive techniques, and we haven't looked at counseling strategies for handling difficulties. But before we can do that, we must be able to connect with people about what they normally experience as good or bad. Many modern astrologers try to avoid speaking about bad things in particular (whether functionally bad or morally bad). But I have often found that clients—and astrologers in their everyday lives—appreciate honesty about these conventional goods or evils. Often clients already know what is going wrong, and they are better served by having us recognize it *astrologically*.

CHAPTER 5: HAPPINESS AND
ASTROLOGICAL COUNSELING

Traditional astrologers were very concerned about human happiness. But what is happiness, exactly? In this chapter I'll describe two important philosophies of happiness that can be used even today to understand the chart and help clients. Each one has its good and bad points, but I won't try to convince you that one is better than another—besides, there are other alternatives.

The most important thing to understand is that while happiness involves emotions and moods, it is not primarily an emotion. Rather, happiness is a state of affairs in which a person is able to flourish: living well and doing well. But views differed on what counts as the good life or what counts as good or bad, and on what the emotional life of a happy person would be like. You may have a lot of external, conventional goods like wealth and children, but to actually be happy requires a certain excellent *state of character*, in which we properly fulfill certain psychological features and skills as humans and in society. I'll explain below what I mean.

Happiness Type 1: Aristotle and conventional goods

Aristotle's value theory fits very well with our normal sense of a birth chart. As I said in the last chapter, the meanings of the houses map out conventional goods and evils, such as wealth or slavery. Aristotle believes that to be happy we must try to maximize these goods and minimize the evils: according to our normal understanding, homeless and anonymous and sick people are less likely to be happy (or be *able to* be happy) than those who have at least some wealth, status, and health. But Aristotle also recognized that we don't have complete control over whether we can get or avoid these things—we are still subject to luck or Fortune (see Chapter 11). That's why it's important to have a good education and character, live in a just society, and so on, so that as many people as possible are able to learn skills and have positive opportunities.

So when we look at a chart in this spirit, the first thing we can see is the extent to which someone's chart exhibits these conventional goods and evils: does the chart show many good friends? Or are their disruptions in the home? We can also look at the lords of the houses: if the lord of a typically good house is in a very poor condition, it can show a problematic area of life. For instance, if the lord of the tenth house is in the sixth, then the person may have a stable career, but it will likely come about through obscurity, labor, and little recognition. All of these things affect the Aristotelian good life.

On the other hand, Aristotle makes it very clear that these things are not enough to create happiness or unhappiness. Happiness is a state of the *soul*, and results from how the soul manages choices and emotions *about* these external goods. A rich person may be miserable because the state of her soul is imbalanced and chaotic; a rather poor person could be happy because he has a very strong and balanced character. So what makes one's character good or bad? For Aristotle, a key notion is that of the "mean." When we confront conventionally good or bad things and have emotions about them, it's important that we use (1) rational judgment to reach (2) an appropriate mean in our emotions, and that (3) these choices become habitualized. It's not enough to make an occasional good choice or feel appropriate emotions: to be happy we must habituate ourselves to live a life according to this rational judgment and mean, in order to gain a firm character. The best state of character with respect to some emotion and situation, is called a "virtue"—so for example, there are virtues concerned with money, with pleasures, with anger, and so on.

Let me give you two simple examples. Suppose I have had a couple of martinis and want another one. Having fun while drinking with friends can be considered a good, and so I want to continue doing it, and I know I'll have pleasure when I drink it. But there are two things to consider. First, there is a balance of pleasure and pain involved. I mustn't be overly pained if I don't have it, and I mustn't be overly excited with pleasure if I do have it. Second, there is the question of whether it is rationally right for me to stop now or keep drinking, depending on other interests and needs in my life. Do I have to get up early (which suggests I shouldn't have it)? Or am I at a friend's wedding at a tropical resort, with no other responsibilities (which suggests I could easily have it)? These questions have to do with the virtue of temperance, which covers pleasures and pains with respect to drinking, food, and sex. Ideally, I have habituated myself so that I can stop drinking with a minimum of pain if I need to, or I can keep going without feeling greedy for pleasure if I need to. Inexperienced drinkers have a harder time figuring this sort of thing out, while experienced and balanced drinkers don't. The experienced drinker who is easily able to make a decision and have these balanced emotions, probably has this virtue of temperance.

Then there is courage, which is a mean involving feelings of fear and confidence in dangerous situations: the courageous soldier knows how to keep fighting despite the danger, but also knows when it's time to retreat. But he does not succumb either to foolhardy overconfidence or terror, and he knows how to act skillfully based on these emotions and the needs of the situation.

But most of us have these virtues in only a couple of areas of life. There are two contrasting conditions in which we do not hit the mean or proper balance in emotion and action. The first is a "vice." Vices are states in which we consistently hit an extreme instead of a well-judged mean. A soldier who consistently and deliberately follows only his confident feelings, becomes a foolhardy person; one who always follows fear is a coward. A raging alcoholic follows the pleasure of drinking (for many reasons, I'm sure) and feels extremely pained when he is not drinking. Anorexics have become habituated to hating food and drink. Someone who feels much distress at not having a second dessert cannot be as happy and balanced as someone who feels little or no distress.

The second condition is called "lack of self-control." Most of us fall into this category in a number of areas. Here, there is a real inconsistency and confusion in judgments, emotions, and actions. Most of us have had the experience of suddenly throwing caution to the wind and having a few more drinks, and paying for it the next day with a hangover at work. Bulimia is a good example of this condition, with its wild contrasts of gorging and purging. Someone who constantly vacillates inappropriately between confidence and fear is another example.

So in Aristotle's philosophy, we have states of a stable mean (virtues), of stable extremes (vices), and inconsistent vacillation. If we apply this to the chart, we can use dignities and other planetary conditions to identify habits and people that exhibit these traits. For instance, we might compare a planet in its domicile to someone with a virtue; in its exaltation, to someone that might have a vice of excessive self-confidence; someone in fall as having certain vices or even lack of self-control, because planets in fall often show a struggle to be noticed, which can lead to extreme behaviors (see Chapter 8). A planet in a difficult aspect to Saturn might show problems in self-worth, though it might simply be an area of life whose conventional goods are hard to come by. Benefics tend to show balanced states, while malefics often show extremes. There could be many ways to look at these conditions, but these are a few of my suggestions.

Happiness Type 2: The Stoics and selective values

Stoic value theory is partly a response to Aristotelian values, so it was important to deal with Aristotle first. The Stoics have insights into values and emotions that Aristotle does not really bring out, but once we do so we can see that Stoicism has a more "spiritual" dimension to it that values liberation, personal confidence, and a positive emotional engagement with life. Let me explain a few basic points about Stoic value theory, and then contrast it with Aristotle. This will help you understand what is at stake in their worldviews.

The Stoic picture of the universe starts with the idea that the universe is the Divine Mind. God does not stand outside the universe, God *is* the universe. This has three important consequences. First, it means that all things are connected in an integrated, organic cosmos. Second, it means that the universe is intelligently organized and managed—not from outside, but from within. Everything that you and I are and do and think, is ultimately part of, and carries out, the activity of the Divine Mind. Third, this means that all things are determined and fated to be what they are, and do what they do, in the course of the universe's activity. Put another way, everything acts inevitably according to its nature: there is nothing that is "not supposed to happen," from the cosmic perspective.

This last part may be a bit hard to swallow, so let me explain it a bit more. From the cosmic perspective, everything inevitably happens how it does, precisely because things cannot help doing what they do, and everything in the world is implicated somehow in how things happen. A cloud follows its nature and sometimes releases rain, a stone falls, and so on. From our limited human perspective, we cannot really tell exactly how things will happen, because we can't describe the entire cosmic state at any moment. But we already do know that angry people—because of their character—will do this or that. A loving person loves. If I tell you to carry an umbrella because it will rain, but you're the type of person not to listen to advice, then you will not bring an umbrella and you will get wet. There is no sense blaming the universe for your getting wet, because the clouds acted according to their nature, and so did you. But maybe I could convince you to carry an umbrella:

in that case, your state of mind would have changed, and you would have behaved differently.

Now, the universe is set up in such a way that there are inevitable clashes between things (like your desire to be both stubborn and not get wet, and the cloud's pouring down rain). In the human case these clashes are especially stark, because most people have mental distortions about who they really are and what they are trying to do. These distortions of understanding result in unhappiness. So on the Stoic view, the goal of life—happiness—involves "living in accordance with nature" and having "a smooth flow of life." This means that we are supposed to align ourselves with our true natures and the cosmic nature, so as to embrace the goodness of the universe, without getting disturbed by what happens when other things act according to *their* natures.

Here's where Stoic value theory comes in. Recall that for Aristotle, normal things like wealth and reputation are goods, and we should try to maximize them, even though he also says that happiness officially derives from our mental ability to manage them (and our emotions about them) correctly. The Stoics take a stricter view: *only* the state of your mind and emotions is responsible for happiness, and these external things *are not* good *or* evil. Instead of having moral value, they have what the Stoics call "selective" value. Instead of wealth being good, it's something that under normal circumstances you should "select"; but in other circumstances, you should "de-select" it. What Aristotle calls "good," the Stoics call "in accordance with nature"; what he calls "bad," they call "not in accordance with nature."

This may all sound weird, but here's how it works in practice. If you think that wealth is a good, then you are making it responsible (in part) for your happiness. You want it. You desire it. When you get wealth you are pleased, but when you don't have it you may be in despair. That makes you a slave to things that you cannot really control, and often makes you overreact either with joy (when you get them) or despair (when you don't get them). In other words, if you assign moral value to things that are not you and don't really belong to you, then you automatically become emotionally invested in them and act as though they should really be part of you. This is not only a false view of what really belongs to you, but puts you on an emotional rollercoaster which forces you to negotiate opposing emotions—that's what Aristotle is talking about when he speaks of the mean, and of managing emotions.

But if you change your value system so that things like wealth only have "selective" value, then it immediately detaches you emotionally from things, so that you are not a slave to them. You are able to feel more centered and calm in yourself, both when you get them but also when you lose them. Suppose a man assigns moral value to his beloved car as something good. But one day he finds a dent in the door. He is devastated, is put in a bad mood, feels a sense of loss, and maybe takes it out on someone else later in the day (this sort of thing happens to children all the time). Now, if he were an Aristotelian, he would try to negotiate his feelings of anger so they are coordinated with the importance of the car: the car is a good thing but not a supremely important one, and likewise a dent is an evil, but only a minor one. So maybe he gets only a little angry or a little sad. But from the Stoic perspective, this is not a case of well-managed anger, it's a case of someone with distorted values who is letting an inanimate object control his mind— it's a kind of emotional sickness. He should do what he can to "select" keeping his car safe, but not believe that this is ultimately in his power or able to control his happiness. Unfortunately, such a man probably doesn't just think a car is good, but he is emotionally a slave to many other things in the same way—let's hope they don't get damaged!

Most of humanity is subject to these delusions. For the Stoics, this allows them to say something that might come as a shock in this day of "owning our emotions" and believing that "every feeling is valid." Unlike most people (and Aristotle), the Stoics do not believe that there are fully pre-given emotions like anger, fear, and lust. Instead, all emotions derive from value judgments. Behind every emotion is some value judgment that makes us either go for something, avoid it, or react in our soul when we either have it or lack it. But since value judgments can be true or false, this means that *emotions can be false or true.* Suppose I think something like wealth is an actual good: this sets up an impulse to go for it. But this desire is a false desire, since my judgment about the intrinsic goodness of wealth is false. Now suppose I obtain wealth: this sets up an irrational swelling of pride in my soul, because I think I've gotten something that is really mine and will make me happy: this too is a false emotion.

Now, you might get the idea that the Stoics are against emotions. This is a common misunderstanding. In fact, Stoics advocate changing your value system so that, instead of being a slave to external things and experiencing the rollercoaster of emotions (or trying to find a mean between competing emotions), you transform your bad emotions into what they call the "good feelings." The good feelings emerge when you find the source of happiness in yourself, assign selective value for other things, and start to embrace the whole cosmos as part of your life—or rather, you embrace your life as something integrated with the cosmos. In this way, the Stoics say you can rise *spiritually above* conventional values.

Let me give you some examples of these emotions from authentic Stoic texts. In the class of emotions that have to do with going for something, the "normal" false emotions include anger, lust, cravings of all sorts, and the love of riches. But the "true" Stoic good feelings would involve kindness, generosity, warmth, and affection. False emotions that involve avoiding or fearing things involve hesitance, anguish, shame, superstition, and terror. But the corresponding Stoic emotions are respect and cleanliness. Cleanliness? What could that mean? My sense is that it is like maintaining a clean house: having a calm avoidance of things that could pollute your sense of self-integrity and peace of mind.

I hope you can see that this way of slowing down and detaching yourself emotionally from things not in your control, allows you to be confident and engaged in the world, having sympathy and generosity for other people, and not getting thrown by what life presents. A Stoic embraces but tries to improve the world we live in, realizing that sometimes he must select certain things, while deselecting others, even though these are not what normal people would call good or bad. The two main differences between Aristotelian and Stoic emotions are these: (1) Aristotle believes that some emotions are mainly *irrational and pre-given*, whereas the Stoics believe that they result from *value judgments*; and (2) Aristotle believes we must *manage* and *balance* emotions, whereas the Stoics believe we should *transform* them.

Astrological Counseling

Both the Aristotelian and Stoic ethical systems are compatible with astrological prediction, and are equally able to see the same events and feelings in an astrological figure. But their understanding of human nature, values, and happiness, causes them to view those events and feelings in different moral terms. Consequently, an astrologer who takes one or the other view will offer different sorts of counsel to a client. Although each school of thought wants to (a) offer paths of action to clients and (b) help clients prepare for events, each will do so in a different way and with different expectations of how the client can fare. Aristotelians will counsel the management of emotions about things that are really crucial to our happiness, whereas Stoics will counsel the transformation of our values, and the wise selection or de-selection of those same things. Both schools will advise us to take action, to do certain things and avoid certain things, using delineation and prediction to prepare clients. But the attitude we take towards all this can make all the difference. Here are some steps I suggest when looking at a chart:

Evaluate conventional goods and evils. Here, we can use normal in-terpretation techniques to evaluate the presence of conventional goods and evils (or things in accordance with nature or not). What is the client's social status? Does he or she have friends, and of what sort? How will the client's children fare? How will the relationships be? In this way we can help people prepare for events that are not wholly in their control. This includes doing electional charts for important events, so as to maximize conventional goods or things in accordance with nature. Or, suppose that you see a chart with a lot of planets in detriment, or with lots of cadent planets: these charts suggest either events and plans that start out well but are not long-lasting, or lives where there doesn't seem to be a lot of energy and momentum. Your ability to connect with the client on the level of values will help you form strategies to help them.

Evaluate typical mental and emotional abilities. Both modern and traditional astrology have techniques for this, often involving the Ascendant and its lord, Mercury, and the Moon. What sort of balance is there between the client's emotions and appetites, and rational faculties? What values does the client have, and how do his or her beliefs trigger emotional reactions and affect his or her ability to cope with life? Here we can identify the default ways in which people respond intellectually and emotionally to life, so as to recommend a moderation in goods and emotions, or switching to selective values and emotional transformation. But in no case should we recommend mere passivity and claims of victimhood. Instead, we ought to encourage clients to make conscious choices about things, owning and strengthening their power with respect to emotions and their sense of confidence and self-integrity.

Prediction and preparation. No one is born a sage. But prediction can play an important role in counseling, because it allows people to cultivate preparedness, patience, and calm for people confronting future events. It allows us to have some critical distance from our lives so that we can realistically appraise what will happen and what it means for us, as well as realizing that anything that happens from year to year is only a temporary phase in the cosmic process.

PART II: TECHNIQUES AND CONCEPTS

CHAPTER 6: PLANETS AND OTHER BODIES

In natal work, many traditionalists today stick to the seven ancient planets and their rulerships, and almost never acknowledge points such as a vertex or Black Moon. But some also use the outer planets and even asteroids. From my own observation, it seems that my friends who use outer planets and asteroids do so because they learned them when studying modern astrology, and still find them useful. But I have also found a common theme: almost all traditionalists maintain traditional rulerships, and treat outer planets and asteroids only as secondary bodies or for amplifying details—*not* as primary things to consider. In terms of rulerships, then, Jupiter still rules Pisces, Saturn still rules Aquarius, and Mars still rules Scorpio. And when looking at a chart, many traditionalists will only pay attention to an outer planet or asteroid if it happens to fall within about a degree of some other planet or point that is important. So for example, if Uranus is in your natal 11th but is far from the cusp or any ancient planet, it is often ignored. But if the lord of the Ascendant (the planet ruling the rising sign) is in a very tight square to some outer planet or right on a key asteroid, then that other body might be important for matters of the 1st house or the native's character or life purpose. In this sense, the outer planets and asteroids are something less than a true planet, but something more than a fixed star.

I'll say more about rulerships and dignities in Chapter 8, but here is a scheme from Abū Ma'shar that I find interesting:[6]

---

[6] See his *Book of Religions and Dynasties* I.1.

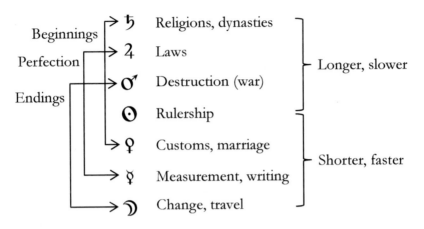

Figure 6: Planets' relationship to society (Abū Ma'shar)

This scheme is a kind of social vision of the planets. The superior (upper) planets signify long-term developments and epochal events, while the inferior (lower) planets signify more short-term ones. Moreover, each planet in the upper group correlates with and needs one in the lower group, so as to make it "real" and practical. So Saturn and Venus both signify foundations and beginnings: Saturn establishes political systems and dynasties, while Venus indicates foundational customs and relationships between people. Jupiter signifies the systems of law and morality that bring the basic ideas of a political system or religion to completion, while Mercury codifies and preserves them through writing (he also indicates literal or figurative "measurement" in the sense of *understanding* and explaining and accounting for what the true and completed natures of things are). Mars and the Moon indicate changes, shifts, and the breakdown of what has come before: Mars through war, the Moon through daily change and travel. In the middle stands the Sun, who signifies rulers acting on behalf of and because of the higher things, and who take a hand in ruling over the lower things.

Note that Saturn especially plays the role of generational or even epochal influences: instead of using outer planets to track trends across generations, traditional astrologers used the Persian theory of astrological history I mentioned in Chapter 1. The main idea is this: if we track Saturn-Jupiter conjunctions over time, we see that they tend to cluster in the same element for about 240 years: about every 20 years, Saturn and Jupiter conjoin in a sign of a certain element (say, a fiery sign), and will then conjoin 20 years later in another sign of the same element; 20 years later, the same thing. After a couple of hundred years, their conjunction will suddenly change into the next element (in this case, the earthy signs), with numerous conjunctions throughout that element, until they change again. The first conjunction in an elemental series is called "the conjunction of the change," and it marks changes in world history and religions. By tracking the lesser conjunctions every 20 years (and applying other predictive techniques), we get more information about generational changes and political shifts. This is not to say that the outer planets can't show similar things. But traditional astrology has a ready-made theory and set of techniques for this, which are worth looking at.

This alternative way of looking at generational change leads me to another point: in traditional astrology, *all planets are also personal planets*. Every planet has associations with either some aspect of the soul (Venus for love, the Moon for the body and associated emotions) or people in our lives (Saturn for an older male relative, the Moon for the mother), even though certain planets are especially used when looking at someone's personal psychology (Mercury and the Moon). We don't necessarily group planets as being either personal or impersonal (or generational) planets.

In fact, I think most modern astrologers work this way, too. But I have noticed a puzzling habit among modern astrologers: although the outer planets are often called impersonal or generational, they are often the *first* things that modern people notice in a birth chart, and are used to explain all sorts of very personal features of life and details of events—even the very long-lasting transits of outer planets are often used to explain virtually everything. Many people let the outer planets monopolize the chart, so that something that might normally be assigned to Jupiter (say, spirituality) or violence (Saturn, Mars) are given to Neptune, Uranus, and Pluto, leaving the ancient planets with much less to do.

I don't currently use outer planets, but there's no reason you couldn't try treating the outers and asteroids differently: try to notice them only when they are about a degree from an angle or ancient planet, and force yourself to make the most out of the ancient planets instead. You might be surprised to find that you rarely need outer planets, and when you do use them in this restricted way they will be more interesting and helpful to you.

CHAPTER 7: SIGNS

You might find it strange that even the signs could be treated differently in traditional astrology, but it's true. The two main differences I see are these: first, traditionally the signs are not viewed primarily in psychological terms; second, there is an expanded and rich array of categories for the signs that are used in certain circumstances. Before saying anything more, let me show you three short descriptions of Capricorn from traditional texts:[7]

"The sign of Capricorn is a domicile of Saturn, but the kingdom[8] of Mars in its twenty-eighth degree, but the slavery[9] of Jupiter in the fifteenth. However, its first face [is] that of Jupiter, the second that of Mars, the third that of the Sun. Its nature: cold and dry, earthy, melancholic, an acidic taste, feminine, nocturnal, convertible,[10] wintry, its beginning increasing the day, of a round shape, incomplete [in figure];[11] of two wills and natures (for the first part [is] earthy and dry, sometimes powerful over beasts and sterile [men], the second part watery, flowing,[12] of many children, foul);[13] having grassy land and what is like grass;[14] of a good life, a mediocre voice, tending to anger, cautious,[15] panicky, sad, libidinous, [dark]. In a man, the knees. In lands, Ethiopia and the banks of the Indus, [Makrān, Sind, Oman and Bahrain] and Hind up to the Hijāz."[16]

"Of regions, Capricorn has Ethiopia and Makrān and Sind, and the river of Makrān, and the shore of the sea which follows those regions, and Oman, and the two seas[17] up to Hind, its boundaries up to Sind, and the Ahwaz, and the boundaries of the land of the Romans. And of

---

[7] I will omit some of the footnotes that originally appeared in my translation of these texts.
[8] Or, "exaltation."
[9] Or, "fall."
[10] Or, "movable," nowadays often called "cardinal."
[11] Reading with the Ar. for "jealous," but jealousy could make sense for a Saturnian sign.
[12] *Fluxilis*, as water flows. But it also has bad moral connotations, and part of Capricorn is indeed known as "lecherous."
[13] The Ar. has the last part of Capricorn also indicating birds.
[14] The Ar. adds "insects of the earth."
[15] The Ar. adds, "master of stratagem."
[16] Abu Ma'shar, *The Abbreviation of the Introduction* I.63-69, in my *ITA* I.3.
[17] Lit., "Bahrain."

places it has palaces and portals and gates and gardens, and every irrigated place, also rivers and the flowing down of waters and rivers, and irrigation canals, and ancient cisterns[18] and every riverbank above which there are trees, and a shore at which there are plantings, and places of dogs and foxes, also wild beasts and predatory animals, and the lodging-places or staying-places of foreigners and resident slaves,[19] and places in which fires are lit."[20]

"And it signifies a man who knows how to lead a good life, and one easy to anger, and who knows well how to provide and look after his own affairs, and even those of others. And he will know well how to counsel those seeking advice from him; and a clever man in good things and bad, if he wished; and likewise a man who is often and easily saddened."[21]

It doesn't look too familiar, does it? True, there are indications for elements and gender and some personality traits. (Bonatti's personality traits are probably based on a Capricorn Ascendant: the domicile rulership by Saturn gives practicality and sober advice and sorrow, and the exalted rulership by Mars shows up as quickness to anger.) But then there are other things like geography, architecture and types of grass, astronomical considerations like the length of daylight, animals, body parts, fertility, tastes, and so on. What is going on here?

What's going on is this. Although some characteristics of the signs are drawn directly from such things as the shape of the zodiacal animal (such as Leo indicating wild beasts) or from the position of the movable ("cardinal") sign when Aries rises (such as Capricorn being a southern sign), the signs are primarily background conditions and structures for the planets in them and the house they occupy. Sometimes this means the sign will indicate a physical place, which is useful in horary and mundane astrology; sometimes it refers to the overall style of energy in light of which the houses and planets operate,

---

[18] John of Spain reads, "fishponds" (Lat. *piscinas*).
[19] Or, "residents and slaves."
[20] Abu Ma'shar, *The Great Introduction to the Science of the Judgments of the Stars* VI.9.1259-68, in my *ITA* I.3.
[21] Bonatti's *Book of Astronomy* II.2 Ch. 21 (p. 81), also known as *Bonatti on Basic Astrology*, p. 81.

which is useful in every branch. Here's what I'd say are the four major traditional ways of approaching the signs:

- They act as places of dignity for certain planets. See Chapter 8.
- They indicate elemental qualities (triplicities) and styles of those energies (the quadruplicities). These can translated into psychological characteristics in certain situations. I'll mention this below.
- They have specialized indications that are often only relevant for specific circumstances: being four-footed, being royal, fully voiced, "prolific" or having many children, being northern, and so on. I'll omit this here because it would get us too far into interpretive techniques.
- How they rise and set provides a structure for certain predictive techniques, such as ascensional times and primary directions. Appendix A has more information on sources for these techniques.

To give some quick examples, a planet in Capricorn may or may not be in one of its own dignities; in a horary chart for a conflict it may be important that Capricorn is a movable sign, and for a lost object that it is an earthy sign or indicates certain physical locations; in questions of fertility, it matters that it is not one of the prolific signs; when interpreting an eclipse or comet in Capricorn, its relation to certain regions of the world will be important. Only sometimes do the personality traits of Capricorn become relevant, particularly when it is on the Ascendant.

One interesting point to note is that the older astrologers did not use the triplicities (the elements) as often as we do for standard delineations—though that changed somewhat in the Renaissance and Early Modern periods. Instead, they usually emphasized the quadruplicities (nowadays called the "modes"). Take a look at the following quotes from ibn Ezra and Sahl:

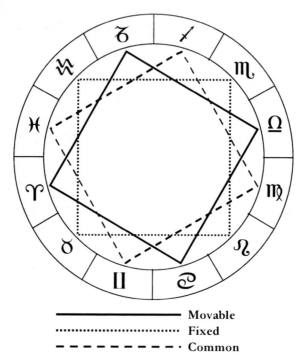

Movable ————————
Fixed ••••••••••••••••••••••
Common — — — — — — — —

Figure 7: Quadruplicities

"If a planet were in a fixed sign, it denotes everything fixed [and] stable. And if it were in a movable one, it will be transformed. And if it were in a common one, it signifies a stable thing, partly [stable] and partly changeable."[22]

"If planets were in fixed signs, they signify fixity—that is, firmness and the stability of matters concerning which the question comes to be. And if they were in common signs, they signify the loosenings of matters and repetitions, and other things will be attached to that matter (or some such other thing). And if they were in movable signs, they signify the speed of the conversions or changes of matters into good or evil."[23]

---

[22] Abraham ibn Ezra, *The Beginning of Wisdom* VIII.47.
[23] Sahl bin Bishr, *The Fifty Judgments* 46.

One little point about vocabulary: what we normally call "cardinal" signs today were called "movable, convertible, turning," and so on, because they show quick changes and movements. The fixed signs were sometimes called the "firm" or "solid" signs. What we call the "mutable" signs were usually the "common" or "double-bodied" signs, because these signs show a sharing of two qualities held together in common by the sign. Ptolemy gave an early explanation of this based on the seasons: the first month of a season (movable) shows a more dramatic change from the previous one, the second month (fixed) shows an intensification and solidification of that season's weather and temperatures, and the last month (common) wobbles back and forth between the current season, and hints of the new one.

So generally, the quadruplicities were used to show a kind of structural style of energy within each element and for each planet. This was used by traditional astrologers to talk about whether a native's life implies more changes, stability, or wavering. For example, if the primary planets and places in a natal chart (the Ascendant, luminaries, lord of the Ascendant, perhaps angular planets) were in common signs, this can show someone whose life encounters a lot of repetitions, going back and forth, indecisiveness (perhaps because they can see things from many different perspectives), and so on. I'll give examples of this in my case study (Chapter 14).

CHAPTER 8: USING DIGNITIES

Traditional astrology uses a lot of what are often called "dignities and debilities."[24] A dignity is a kind of ownership or rulership, and when a planet is in a place of dignity it usually shows some kind of competence and consistency in what it indicates. Debilities show different ways in which affairs become less organized, or obscure, or unsteady and uncertain.

I'm sure you've heard of the two main dignities or rulerships, which are:

1. **Domicile**. This refers to a planet ruling a sign, such as Mars ruling Aries. Mars is the lord or "domicile lord" of Aries. When Mars is in Aries, he is "in his own domicile."
2. **Exaltation**. This refers to a planet which is exalted in a sign, such as the Sun being exalted in Aries. The Sun is the "exalted lord" of Aries. When the Sun is in Aries, he is "in his own exaltation," or he "is exalted."

These are the ones I will talk about in this chapter. But traditionally, there are *three* other main kinds of dignity. They are often used only for specific purposes and techniques, and as dignities they are considered "weaker" than the domicile or exaltation:

3. **Triplicity**. All three signs of a given element (say, the fiery signs) are ruled by a set of three planets, which may not be their domicile or exalted lords.
4. **Bound** (often called a "term"). Each sign is subdivided into five unequal bits, each one of which is ruled by a planet—but the Sun and Moon do not rule any bounds.
5. **Face** or **decan**. Each sign is divided into three equal portions of 10°, each of which is ruled by one of the seven traditional planets.

The main idea behind a dignity is that each planet has *management responsibility* for the areas of the zodiac it rules. So no matter where Aries is in the chart, Mars is responsible for managing whatever Aries means, because he is

---

[24] I should say up front that I don't think "debility" is a very helpful term. It means "weakness," but not every debility is best understood in terms of being weak. Nor is "debility" a true counterpart to "dignity," which means "worthiness" and refers to social rank and responsibility.

the domicile lord of Aries. If Aries is the tenth house, then Mars is trying to manage tenth-house affairs; if the fifth, then he rules fifth-house affairs. Likewise, no matter where Aries is, the Sun is its exalted lord and has his own management responsibility.

Following is a diagram that shows you the domicile and exaltation rulerships:

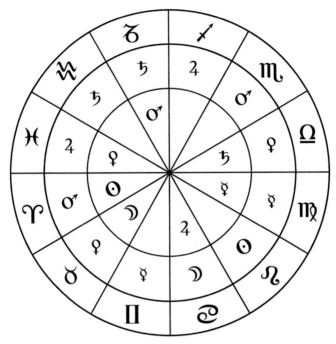

Figure 8: Planetary domiciles (outer) and exaltations (inner)

It helps to imagine that each sign is like a household (in fact, the signs are the "houses" or "domiciles" of the planets). If you are one of the heads of your household, then you are responsible for supporting and managing your household. If you are sick, or away on vacation, or something happens to you, then it effects your domestic life and anyone living there. Just so, if Aries is your tenth house, then Mars manages your reputation and actions and career, and what he is doing in the chart affects those things. He will always be in some sign of the chart or other, in aspect or out of aspect with some planet, in some beneficial or difficult condition: so as his situation changes, so those matters change. A lot of what we do when looking at the natal chart, is understanding what is happening to a house and its domicile lord.

The difference between a domicile lord and an exalted lord is roughly this. Imagine a university department, which has a department chair and a chief administrative secretary. The department chair is like the exalted lord: he makes some executive decisions and is officially responsible for the department, but he is not a really hands-on person in day-to-day affairs. If he wants to send a letter, he might not know where the stamps are kept; or he might not know whom to call if the computer breaks down. But as we all know, the administrative secretary is often the one who really runs the show. If you need something practical done, if you need a phone number or need to know what a department policy is, or what your degree requirements are, she knows what to do. She is like the domicile lord.

These analogies can be extended to other areas of life: the exalted lord is like the owner of a restaurant, but the domicile lord is the manager who actually runs it and brings in the money. Many wealthy people (exalted lords) hire household managers (domicile lords) to pay bills, manage the calendar, hire construction workers and manage the cleaning service. In traditional astrology, these domicile lords or household managers are the real powers in the chart. For the most part, we do not use exalted lords when delineating a house topic.

But here is something very crucial: how well a domicile lord (or any planet) is doing, how organized and efficient and confident it is, depends to a great extent on whether or not it is in any of its dignities. Let's take Mars: he rules Aries, and in any chart he's going to be its domicile lord and try to manage its affairs. But he will always be in one sign or another, and it might not be one he rules or feels comfortable in. If he is in a sign he rules by domicile (Aries or Scorpio), then he will be more comfortable, and you'll see more constructive and efficient Martial qualities come out. But if he is in his detriment or fall, or is peregrine (or even a combination of these), we get more disorganized and troubled effects which affect the area of life indicated by Aries. Let's look at these three counter-dignities now.

Detriment. The sign of a planet's detriment is always opposite the sign it rules by domicile, so if a planet rules two signs, it has two signs of detriment. For instance, the Sun (the lord of Leo) is in detriment in Aquarius, while Mars (the lord of Aries and Scorpio) is in detriment in both Libra and Taurus. The core meaning of detriment is "corruption," which carries the following basic meanings: disintegration, disunity, lack of control, discomfort or enmity, and even moral corruption (at least, in the eyes of the community). It can also show something that is "alternative" or "countercultural," because it represents the dissolving of standard norms. So if Mars is in the sign of his detriment, his Martial activity and his Martial events will have these characteristics. Imagine the difference between a disciplined, organized, and competent soldier (domicile) and a soldier who lashes out in fear, fights poorly, is antagonistic, clumsy, and so on.

Fall or descension. The sign of fall is always opposite that of exaltation, so that Mars (exalted in Capricorn) is in fall in Cancer; the Sun (exalted in Aries) is in fall in Libra. Since every planet has only one sign of exaltation, each has only one sign of fall. And since there are twelve signs but only seven traditional planets, five signs have no falls in them. The basic image of a planet in fall is someone who has fallen down a well: they may shout and cry, but no one hears them. In social situations, a planet in its own fall usually represents someone disrespected or of low social status. We might also imagine it indicates things of low quality, or even psychological impulses that are hard to access and express well. In addition, it can show something that is socially unusual or alternative because it is something overlooked and not in the mainstream, public eye.

One interesting feature of fall is this: since each planet is trying to be itself, then it will often work harder to express itself: so fall can show a difficulty that someone is trying to overcome. Sometimes this has unpleasant results. Since Mars is a malefic planet, you might think it's good to have him sidelined and ignored. But have you ever tried to ignore a really Martial person? It usually doesn't work: he or she can easily get loud, strident, interrupt, and lash out, all as a strategy for trying to be heard. So we cannot simply look at these counter-dignities at face value, because what we see in a person's life and personality is often their attempt to *overcome* these underlying problems.

Following is a diagram of the signs of detriment and fall, and the planets in them:

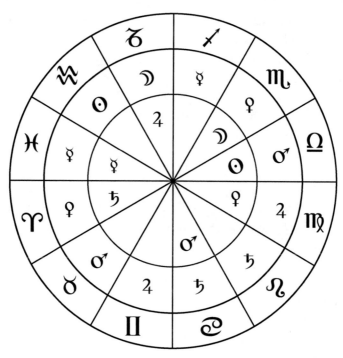

Figure 9: Planetary detriments (outer) and falls (inner)

Peregrine. Lastly, let's look at what it is to be "peregrine." The word in Latin and Arabic really means to be a traveler, stranger, foreigner, or pilgrim. A planet is peregrine when it's in a place where it has no positive dignity at all, such as the Sun in Taurus. It's like being in a foreign land where you hardly speak the language, and you really depend on the good graces of others to get along. You might be confused and lost, or the cheap hotel you wanted is booked, and so on. You might have to stay with people you don't like and where you have little control. Or on the other hand, you might land in just the right spot—but the point is that you don't have the kinds of normal control you enjoy at home. Just so, when a planet is peregrine, its condition and behavior really depend upon what is going on with the domicile lord of that sign. If the lord of the sign is in a favorable house and in one of its own dignities, or some other favorable situation, then the peregrine planet does better: it's as though it has someone taking care of them. But if the lord of the sign is in the opposite conditions, it will be less enjoyable, constructive, and so on.

Some people get confused as to how peregrination fits in with detriment and fall. Remember: being peregrine means *lacking* one of the positive dignities, it doesn't rule out the possibility of being in a *counter-dignity* as well. For instance, the Sun is peregrine in Taurus because he has none of the five dignities there. He is also peregrine in Aquarius for the same reasons, but because he is *also* in detriment in Aquarius, this potentially makes things worse for whatever he signifies in a chart.

When interpreting a planet in a dignity or counter-dignity, here's a hint: for dignities, consider what would be the most organized and constructive (domicile) or exalted and self-confident (exaltation) expressions of those planets, and then ask yourself what would it be like for that planet to be disorganized and so on (detriment) or low-grade and marginalized (fall). Of course you have to take their planetary natures into account. A disorganized Mars will act differently than a disorganized Jupiter.

	Domicile	Exaltation	Detriment	Fall
♈	♂	☉ (esp. 19°)	♀	♄ (esp. 21°)
♉	♀	☽ (esp. 3°)	♂	
♊	☿		♃	
♋	☽	♃ (esp. 15°)	♄	♂ (esp. 28°)
♌	☉		♄	
♍	☿	☿ (esp. 15°)	♃	♀ (esp. 27°)
♎	♀	♄ (esp. 21°)	♂	☉ (esp. 19°)
♏	♂		♀	☽ (esp. 3°)
♐	♃		☿	
♑	♄	♂ (esp. 28°)	☽	♃ (esp. 15°)
♒	♄		☉	
♓	♃	♀ (esp. 27°)	☿	☿ (esp. 15°)

Figure 10: Table of major dignities and corruptions/debilities[25]

---

[25] In traditional texts there is widespread inconsistency between cardinal and ordinal numbers. For example, the exaltation of the Sun is variously given as "nineteen" degrees (19°), and the "nineteenth" degree (18°). My sense is that the authors probably meant "at the end of the nineteenth degree, namely at 19°."

Exercise: Take a look at the following chart and answer the questions below.[26]

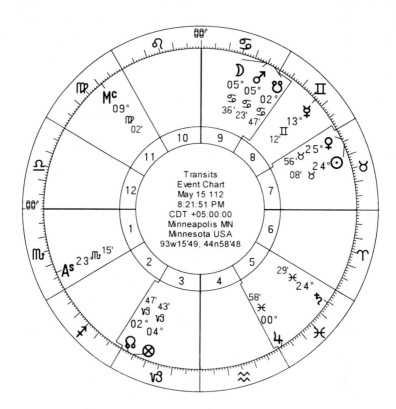

1. Four planets are in their own domiciles in this chart: which are they?
2. Which planet is in its fall?
3. Which two planets are peregrine?
4. Look at Jupiter and his dignity-condition in the fifth house. What do you think this might mean for the children of such a person? Remember to consider the nature of Jupiter in addition to his dignity condition there.

CHAPTER 9: HOUSES

Now let's look at the houses. Just as in modern astrology, these indicate areas of life, and the planets' conditions and natures particularly affect the area of life belonging to the house they are in and rule. Before talking about some special features of traditional houses, let me point out two important differences between some modern approaches and the traditional one.

First, there is no "alphabet" or one-to-one correspondence between houses, signs, and planetary lords. Houses, signs, and planets are distinct. That is to say, the first house does not have the nature of Aries and Mars. The second house does not have the nature of Taurus and Venus. Nor does the fact that Capricorn or Saturn is in some house have anything to do with tenth-house matters—*unless* Capricorn or Saturn happen to be in the tenth house itself, or Saturn actually rules the tenth. Such overlaps are only apparent, and using them will lead to confusion when you interpret a chart. Offhand, I can think of only a couple of instances where traditional astrologers apply these ideas, but they seem to be idiosyncratic and forced—and in one instance, the attempt to draw out these similarities gets dropped after a few examples because the comparison doesn't really work.

Second, the order of houses does not match any evolutionary development. The reason the houses are numbered the way they are, is simply because that's the order in which the signs move clockwise over the horizon: the idea of counterclockwise development through the houses really doesn't make sense, if you look at what the houses mean. Does it make sense that we have children (fifth house) before we have relationships (seventh)? Or that we die (eighth) before we have careers? No. There are modern psychological theories that try to make this sequence work, but to my mind (and to the traditional mind), this involves a misunderstanding and confusion of houses, signs, and planets.

With that in mind, I'd like to point out three useful and important features of traditional houses: (1) some differences in meanings, (2) the use of whole-sign houses, and (3) places that are said to be "strong," "advantageous," "busy," or "conducive to business." There are some current disagreements about the relationship between the last two points, so I'll give you the best short introduction to them I can.

(1) Difference in meanings. Many of the house meanings are identical to modern ones, with four important exceptions. Again, here are the basic traditional house meanings:

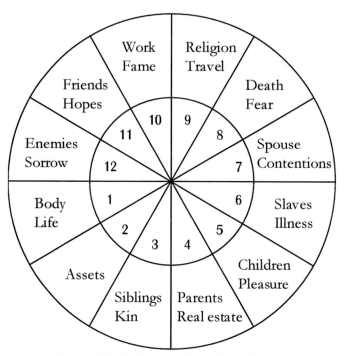

Figure 11: Basic meanings of the houses

If you look around, you'll see that the four places with the greatest differences are the second, sixth, eighth, and twelfth. These places are said to be "in aversion to" or "turned away from" the Ascendant. I'll talk about what that means in the next chapter, but you can see that the meanings of three of them are negative, whereas in modern astrology they are usually positive. Instead of slavery and illness for the sixth, most moderns say that this is a place of "work." In traditional astrology this is not so much a problem, provided that by "work" you really mean *labor* and being a *subordinate*. This is the kind of work for which you get little recognition, because the tenth is the place of recognition. For the eighth, many moderns recognize the spouse's assets, and this is also a traditional meaning. But in no way does it mean "sex" (a fifth house matter) or "transformation" (unless you mean your body's transformation into a corpse!). Likewise, the twelfth house has more to do with experiences that make you more trapped and inhibit your freedom: enemies (especially hidden ones), mistakes, depression, isolation, imprisonment. It might indicate matters of mystery and the occult as well, but it does not refer to spiritual enlightenment because neither Pisces nor Jupiter nor Neptune have an intrinsic relationship to it—those matters belong more to the ninth and the third (which is also a spiritual house in traditional astrology). Finally, the second house has more to do with personal assets and allies—the money and people that actually support you and are ready-to-hand. It cannot mean "values," because values and things we value are all over the chart, and the second has no intrinsic relationship to Venus. I already discussed values in a previous chapter.

So, those are the major differences in meaning, and I'll explore them a bit more in the next chapter. For now, let's turn to house systems.

(2) **House systems and whole-sign houses.** Up until the 1980s, people generally thought that traditional astrology used only the kinds of house systems we recognize today: Placidus, Regiomontanus, Equal, and so on. Indeed, ancient and medieval people also did recognize Porphyry and Alchabitius Semi-Arcs, among others. Except for equal houses, these systems are now often called "quadrant" houses, because in one way or another they result from dividing the quadrants between the axial degrees (the Ascendant, Midheaven, Descendant, and Imum Coeli or IC) into three parts: thus the area between the degree of the Midheaven and that of the Ascendant contains unequal spaces called the tenth, eleventh, and twelfth houses. Because of the obliquity of the ecliptic, different systems and latitudes sometimes yield more than one house cusp on a sign, and some signs can be wholly contained or "intercepted" within two cusps.

But translators of older material have discovered that there was an older and probably original house system, now called "whole-sign" houses. In this case, each *sign* is equivalent to a house. So while the axial degrees are still used for important purposes, there are no intermediary cusps at all, and no intercepted signs. Take a look at the diagram below:

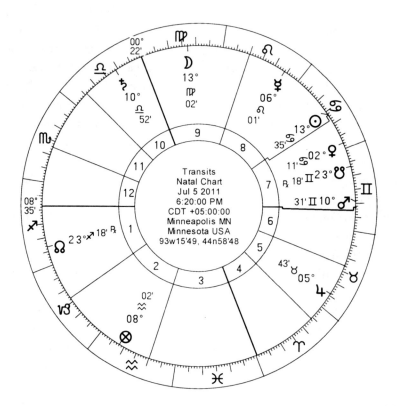

This chart is cast for Alchabitius Semi-Arcs, a popular medieval quadrant system. You can see that the Ascendant is on 8° Sagittarius, and so the first house reaches from there until 13° Capricorn, containing part of Sagittarius and part of Capricorn. The upper parts of Sagittarius are considered to be in the twelfth house. Pisces and Virgo are wholly intercepted in the third and ninth, and there are two house cusps on Scorpio and Taurus. Venus is considered to be a seventh-house planet because she is contained in the quadrant division that begins at the Descendant in Gemini.

But in whole signs, things are different. Because Sagittarius is the ascending sign, *all* of Sagittarius is the first house, both the parts above the actual rising degree, and the parts below. The first house ends where Sagittarius ends. The second house is the entire second sign, Capricorn, and any planet at all in Capricorn would be a second-house planet—and so on. You can also see that while the Midheaven falls in the eleventh sign (the eleventh whole-sign house), Virgo (the tenth sign) is the tenth whole-sign house. So the Moon in Virgo is a tenth-house planet, and likewise Venus is really an eighth-house planet. There will be no intermediary cusps (except for the sign divisions themselves), and no intercepted signs. Here is what the chart looks like in whole signs:

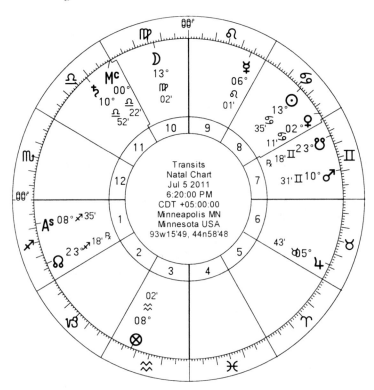

Although the use of quadrant or equal houses is documented for certain early authors, the texts that describe them are controversial and may have introduced these house systems only for certain purposes. For instance, there is evidence that the quadrant houses were mainly used to determine planetary strength or stimulation in a chart—that is, what planets were more powerful or stood out more. I'll mention this again below. But at any rate, the transition from using primarily whole signs to only using quadrant houses came slowly, and seems to have accelerated during the first couple of centuries of the Arabic period.

Many traditionalists, and some modern astrologers, have now embraced whole signs. But as you can imagine, switching to whole signs can be disorienting and scary! In the charts above, it makes a big difference whether Venus is considered a seventh-house planet pertaining to relationships, or an eighth house planet pertaining to death, fear, and so on. I can tell you from my own experience that making this switch often takes time and can lead to a kind of identity crisis and paralysis when looking at charts: what house is a planet really in?

But I can also tell you that once you make the commitment to whole-sign houses, you will probably feel a lot more comfortable and secure. In addition, several features of traditional thought suddenly fall into place when you don't make house meanings overlap with notions of cusps and planetary strength: for instance, the use of aversions and the notion of a planet aspecting its own house (i.e., the sign it rules). I'll talk more about this in Chapter 10.

(3) Advantageous or strong places. As I mentioned, traditional astrologers didn't believe that every planet was equally prominent or "engaged" in the chart. Some planets are considered weaker or more obscure. My own teacher, Robert Zoller, uses the example of a photograph of a group of people. Some people are in front and very clear—your eye is drawn to them immediately. But other people are in the back, partly hidden or even blurry. Likewise at a party, some people linger in the corner, while others are loud and make you pay attention to them. This is not a question of whether these people (or planets) are good or interesting, it's a question of volume and prominence.

Let's look at two versions of this idea, because it leads to a compromise way of talking about planetary strength that combines whole-sign houses and quadrant systems. The first diagram below has eight places that are said to be "advantageous" or "strong." Since this approach is attributed to the possibly mythical Nechepso (see Chapter 1), it must be very ancient.

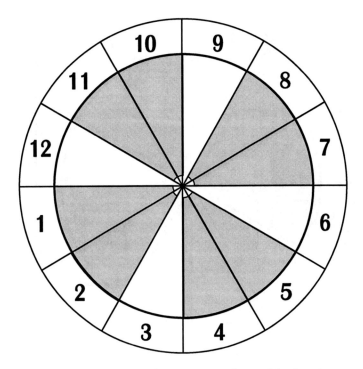

**Figure 12: Eight advantageous places: Nechepso,
Abū Ma'shar, al-Qabīsī**

The gray houses are the places that show "advantage," "strength," being "busy," or "conducive to business" (it's stated differently in different languages). You should immediately see that they are precisely all of the angular houses (first, tenth, seventh, fourth) and the succeedent houses (second, eleventh, eighth, fifth). The remaining houses are cadent, which literally means "falling," as though they are decreasing in power and prominence. According to this approach, planets in these eight advantageous planets are more stimulated, prominent, "strong," and so on. Planets in the angles are the most prominent, while planets in the succeedents are not quite as prominent. Planets in the cadent houses are considered weaker and more obscure, regardless of whether they are also in their own dignities, aspected by powerful good planets, and so on.

But we have to consider an important question: are these whole-sign houses, or quadrant houses? Before trying to answer this, let's look at the next approach:

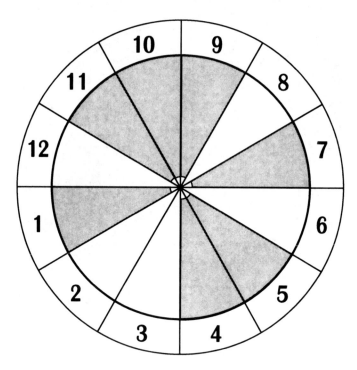

Figure 13: Seven advantageous places (gray):
Timaeus, Dorotheus, Sahl

This diagram has only seven gray places. But can you see something they have in common? They are all either the Ascendant itself, or in aspect to the Ascendant. The eleventh aspects the Ascendant by a sextile, the tenth and fourth by a square, the ninth and fifth by a trine, and the seventh by an opposition. The only house that is configured with the Ascendant but not gray is the third, which is kind of an ambiguous house traditionally. Here then, if a planet is in the ninth, then it is considered advantageous or busy, and so on. This was not true for the previous diagram.

Well, are these simply conflicting approaches, or is there a way to combine them? One solution that many traditionalists are adopting now, is this: (a) the seven-place diagram is based on *whole-signs*, and shows planets that are especially available and busy for *the native*, because they are all configured to the Ascendant. But (b) the eight-place diagram is based on *quadrant divisions*, and shows the busy-ness or prominence of the planets *in themselves and with respect to the whole chart*. I think this approach has a lot of promise, but I must emphasize that we are trying to sift through difficult texts and reconstruct what ancient astrologers did. There may be another answer that works better.

Let's look again at the chart I introduced above, and see how this solution might work:

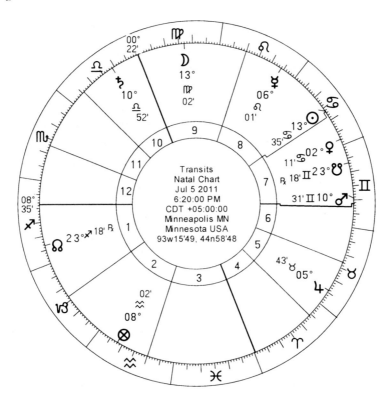

Instead of using the word "house" for everything, let's only call the whole signs "houses," and say that the quadrant divisions (based on the axial degrees) are either "strong" or "middling" or "weak" in their prominence and stimulation. So the area from the degree of the Ascendant at 8° Sagittarius to 13° Capricorn is not the first "house," but it is a strongly stimulated region. The area from 13° Capricorn to 20° Aquarius is not the second house, but it is middling in its stimulation or strength. The area from 20° Aquarius to 0° Aries (where the IC is) is weak in its stimulation or strength. And so on throughout the chart.

If you look at Jupiter, he is in the sixth whole-sign house. This means that he pertains to illness, slavery, stress, pets and small animals, and so on. This house is not one of the advantageous ones according to the seven-place diagram, because it does not aspect the rising sign. But in terms of dynamism or stimulation, he is in a middling region. According to the solution I'm suggesting, he is not necessarily advantageous to the *native*, but he has middling strength in the chart as a whole and with respect to sixth-house matters.

Now look at Saturn. He is in the eleventh whole-sign house, which is an advantageous house to the native. He is also within about 10° degrees of the MC, which means that he is also strongly stimulated in himself or for the chart as a whole. On the other hand, the Moon is in the tenth house (an advantageous place for the native), but she is in a weaker dynamical division: so although she is in a foundational house of the chart and shows something important in life (reputation, profession), she is not as stimulated and prominent as we might want her to be. This means that although she will pertain to tenth-house matters, she might not carry as great a weight as a competing planet such as Saturn (since the degree of the Midheaven still always bears a sense of reputation and profession).

Look now at Venus. She is in the eighth whole-sign house, which is not an advantageous house for the native. But by being in a strongly-stimulated region, she is very active and prominent in the chart and we will have to consider her in the operation of the chart as a whole.

I think this compromise solution is very promising and you may find it very useful in your work. When we look at a chart, we want to see what planets stand out—both for the native herself, based on the seven-place system) and in the chart as a whole (based on the eight divisions from the axial degrees). Just because a planet is available and advantageous or busy *for you*, doesn't mean that its intrinsic power is very great. Likewise, just because a planet is very stimulated and prominent in itself, doesn't mean it is advantageous for you. This can help us evaluate the planets' activity with a bit more subtlety.

Exercise: Answer the following questions, based on the compromise solution I've described. Use whole-sign houses for topics in life, the seven-place diagram with whole signs for places advantageous for the native, and the eight-place diagram with quadrant divisions for the planets' busy-ness and prominence in themselves.[27]

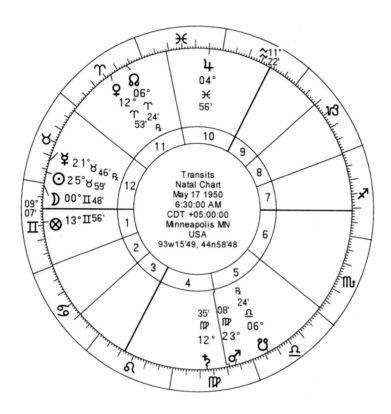

1. What house is the Moon in?
2. What house is Mars in?
3. What house is Jupiter in?
4. State what Saturn's house is, and what dynamic strength he has.
5. What is Mars's dynamical strength?
6. What is Jupiter's dynamical strength?

---

[27] For answers, see Appendix C.

CHAPTER 10: ASPECTS AND AVERSIONS: SIGHT AND BLINDNESS

Now that you've learned a bit about whole signs, I need to introduce you to a further dimension which has to do with aspects and the notion of blindness (and even the unconscious).

Normally, astrologers treat aspects as a planetary relationship by an exact degree, or within a few degrees called an "orb." Take a look at the following chart:

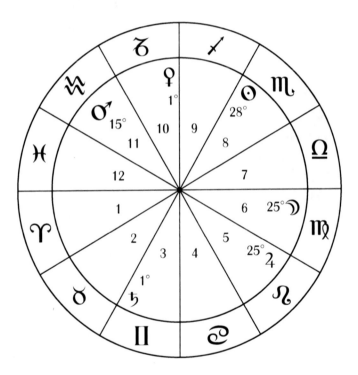

In this example, the Moon is in late Virgo. She is within orbs of a sextile with the Sun in Scorpio, because according to most modern rules a sextile has an orb of 3°. Again, according to modern rules she is within an exact semi-sextile with Jupiter in Leo. She is also within orbs of an out-of-sign trine with Saturn in Gemini, because her trine aspect falls on 25° Taurus, which is within orbs of Saturn at the beginning of the next sign.

In traditional astrology, we treat things a bit differently, and I'll return to this example in just a moment. Traditional astrology distinguishes (1) whole-sign aspects from (2) degree-based aspects proper, often (3) does not allow out-of-sign aspects (though some medieval authors allow out-of-sign conjunctions), which leads to treating the so-called "minor" aspects differently. Let's take these points one-by-one.

(1) Whole sign aspects. It's true that aspects by degree go from one degree to another specific degree—such as when a trine is cast from 15° Leo to 15° Sagittarius. But traditional astrology teaches that the signs as a whole are the basis of the aspects, so that Leo *itself* aspects Sagittarius *itself* by a trine. Since the signs (like whole-sign houses) are treated as distinct units, any planet in some sign will regard or make a whole-sign aspect to any planet in a sign which is configured in the proper way. So, any planet in Virgo aspects any planet in Capricorn by a whole-sign trine, precisely because Virgo itself aspects Capricorn by a trine. The planets' degrees may be very distant, but what matters is the sign itself. In the example above, the Moon aspects Venus by a whole-sign trine, even though their degrees are too far apart for most people to consider that an aspect. A whole-sign aspect is one example of many general *attitudes* or "bearings" (Lat. *habitudo*) that one planet can take toward another.

This kind of whole-sign regard or bearing is attitudinal and has an astrological effect, but it's not like being engaged with someone directly. Imagine that you are sitting next to someone who makes you feel uncomfortable, or that you are with someone whose political views are uncomfortably different from your own: you might not be having a debate, maybe you are ignoring them or only trying to discuss pleasant topics: but there is still a certain unspoken relationship between you, an attitude, a bearing. This is like a whole-sign square. Again, imagine that each sign is like a household in your neighborhood: maybe there is someone down the street you don't know and have never invited over, but you really like how she's developed her garden and treats her kids, and you feel some kind of kinship with her: this is like a whole-sign sextile or trine. Planets that regard each other solely by sign can have this kind of discomfort or friendliness, just as in real life. It's not the most intense kind of relationship, but it's real. If your Moon regards Mars by a whole-sign square, this can show discomfort and friction between what those two planets mean, though it might not become very obvious until they are activated by a predictive technique, and won't be as intense and direct as an aspect based on degrees or orbs.

(2) Aspects proper. What I call an aspect proper is a degree-based aspect: one that takes place within a certain number of degrees often called an "orb." In modern astrology, orbs are normally attached to the kind of aspect itself: so for instance, when studying modern astrology I learned that a trine has an aspect of 6°. So if the Moon in the above chart is in 25° Virgo, then her exact trine is to 25° Capricorn, but any planet within 6° on either side of that would be within her trine aspect.

But in traditional astrology, orbs are normally assigned to *planets*, not the aspects themselves. An exception is a rule in ancient Greek texts, which says that any aspect by degree is only valid within 3°. So in the case of the Moon above, her trine aspect is at 25° Capricorn, but any planet within 3° on either side of that would be in her trine. But by the time of the Arabic and medieval Latin astrologers, different planets got different orbs. Here is a list of traditional orbs from the Persian and Arabic astrologers:

♄	9°
♃	9°
♂	8°
☉	15°
♀	7°
☿	7°
☽	12°

Figure 14: Typical traditional orbs (amount in front and behind)

These orbs are good for the degrees on either side of a planet. So in the above chart, Mars is at 15° Aquarius. He casts an exact sextile ray 60 degrees away, to 15° Aries. But because he has an orb of 9°, any planet within 9° on either side of that would be in his sextile. Of course, if his orb overlapped with that other planet's orb, then the other planet could be further away than 9° and still be considered to be in an aspect within orbs.

You can see that these orbs are sometimes much larger than what we are used to in modern astrology, and you might wonder whether such wide orbs are useful. But remember that the difference between whole-sign and degree-based aspects is really one of intensity: two planets related by sign alone have a looser, less intimate bearing; but planets which engage by degree are beginning to communicate and connect directly with one another: and in

fact, that is precisely what the Arabic term for an applying aspect means: to connect, to communicate.

(3) Aversions and blindness. One effect of this way of looking at regards and aspects, is that for many traditional astrologers, there are no out-of-sign aspects, but there are out-of-sign conjunctions because the bodies of the planets themselves are taken to have a glow about them which allows an interaction across sign boundaries. So according to the older texts, the Moon is not aspecting Saturn in an out-of-sign trine by orbs, because out-of-sign aspects are not allowed. But she is squaring him by whole signs, a rather different kind of aspect!

This leads to a very important concept, "aversion." This is something that will seem very new to modern astrologers, but in fact it is not that different from what you might already know. Classically, planets can only be assembled[28] in the same sign (or in a conjunction by degree), or can regard or aspect each other by a whole-sign sextile, square, trine, or opposition. This leaves four signs out of the picture: the signs on either side of a planet (the second and twelfth signs from it), and the planets in the sixth and eighth from it. The figure below shows what I mean.

In this diagram, Mars is in the tenth whole-sign house, and so he can either be assembled with a planet there, or else be in an aspect with other planets by sextile, square, trine, or opposition (these places are all in gray). But he cannot be in aspect to *any* planet in the eleventh or ninth, or in the third or fifth.[29] These places are said to be "in aversion to" Mars: literally, "turned away" from him.

Now, in modern astrology, there are aspects such as the semi-sextile and the inconjunct, which would allow him to aspect planets in those signs. So, you might think that traditional astrology has a defect, because we do not allow such aspects. But here is the key: *these positions are not aspects, but they still mean something.*

---

[28] That is, in a bodily conjunction. This means being in the same sign, and more intensely within 15° and less (and especially within 3° and less). But as I mentioned, some traditional astrologers allowed out-of-sign conjunctions.

[29] That is, unless we allow out-of-sign conjunctions.

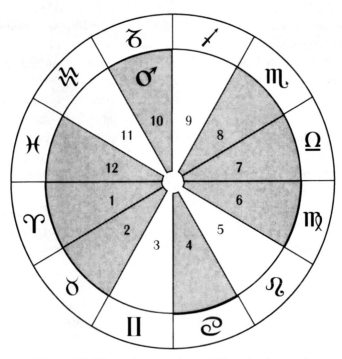

Figure 15: Places in aversion to Mars in the tenth

Remember that the word "aspect" means "to look at." And when planets cast aspects, they are thought to cast rays of light. But looking, seeing, and light, have always been understood in terms of knowledge and control: think of what it means to say, "I see what you mean," or to be "enlightened," or when politicians speak of "looking at an issue," or even that some political issue is "on the table," as though it's something that they will examine and do something about. But when things are in darkness and unseen, they suggest things that are not known, or are ignored, out of reach, and inaccessible—in a psychological context—are in the unconscious or subject to denial.

This is precisely what it means for planets to be in aversion to one another, or especially when a planet is in aversion to a sign which it rules: it means that there is some disconnect, some estrangement, ignorance, not seeing. In some contexts, it can even mean travel (i.e., not being present) or acting without much information. Let me show you two diagrams which illustrate this philosophically and practically:

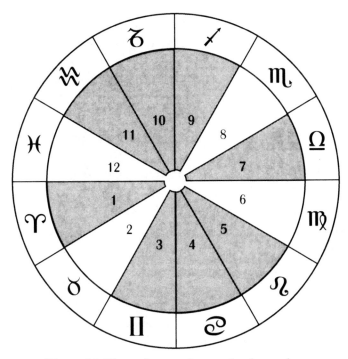

Figure 16: Places in aversion to the Ascendant

In this diagram, let's look at the Ascendant (Aries). By definition, the following houses are in aversion to the Ascendant: the twelfth (Pisces), second (Taurus), sixth (Virgo) and eighth (Scorpio). By being in aversion, these places mean something like ignorance, denial, and so on. Well, what do these very houses mean, traditionally? The twelfth means enemies, specifically hidden enemies; the second means personal assets and possessions, but also one's personal allies; the sixth means illness and also subordinates, slaves, and (medievally) vassals; the eighth means death. If we think about these meanings, we can see how they can show the theme of ignorance: one is ignorant of hidden enemies (twelfth); one also is ignorant and in denial of one's own death (eighth). The second and the sixth might not seem to fit: after all, don't we see and know our own possessions and subordinates? But think about this. In a poor economy, it is often difficult to understand what is really happening with our assets, what their value is and how we can manage them well. Likewise, when speaking of allies, it is sometimes hard to know and trust what their agenda is. For the sixth, we cannot see illness coming, but we likewise are often in the dark about what our subordinates and employees are doing. In the Middle Ages, feudalism was essentially a bargain between a landowner (the Ascendant) and his vassals (the sixth). In exchange for certain favors and land rights, vassals agreed to support the landowner in times of trouble; but you can imagine a lord in his castle, wondering if his vassals are taking advantage of him, what they really have in mind, and if he can count on their support.

If you look at it in another way, the places on either side of the Ascendant represent ignorance about people and things close by (hidden enemies, allies), while the sixth and eighth represent ignorance about things and people apparently very far away or lower in the social order (vassals, death).

So in a certain philosophical sense, places in aversion show real people and events in our lives, but where we are not always sure what the truth is about them. As I said before, these places have no *aspects* to the Ascendant (since aspects imply knowledge and a clear relationship), but they still *mean something*.

What was even more important for traditional authors, was a planet being in aversion to its own sign—that is, not being configured by a whole-sign aspect to its own domicile. Here is an example:

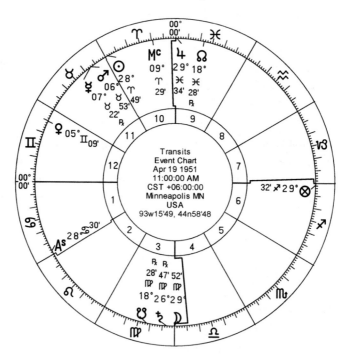

Take a look at Venus. Venus always rules Taurus and Libra, but in this diagram she is in aversion to Taurus (the eleventh house) because it is the adjacent time. Now, because she rules this house, Venus is trying to manage eleventh-house affairs. But she is in aversion to it. What does this mean? Let me give you an intriguing quote from Sahl's book *On Elections*:

"Because a planet which does not aspect its own domicile is like a man absent from his own house, who cannot repel nor prohibit anything from it. Indeed if a planet aspected its own domicile, it is like the master of a house who guards it: for whoever is in the house, fears him, and he who is outside fears to come to it." (*On Elections*, §§23b-c)

In other words, an aspect to one's own domicile shows a two-way relation to one's home and roots. On the one hand, the aspect from the lord shows its protection of the house, providing for its signification, and perfecting it. But this connection also shows that the lord is supported by the house in turn. When the lord is in aversion, it and the house are in need, with the danger of mischief, and the lord being weakened and cut off from its home. *Providing* and *protection* seem to be the key concepts here, and they, too, are related to the notions of home, ownership, and belonging. In this way, whole-sign houses, aspects, and aversions fit neatly together. This is not the case in quadrant-based systems.

Now, Venus being in aversion to the eleventh does not mean that there will always be breaks, differences, and so on in the native's friendships. Sometimes we can only see these things clearly using a timing technique such as a profection (Chapter 13). When this Venus or the eleventh house is activated, we should normally expect these themes to arise. Maybe a friendship is dissolved, maybe the native breaks with old friends and makes new ones, or maybe the friends themselves have erratic experiences. It might also simply mean travel. Or, take another example: suppose the lord of the fourth (family, home) is in aversion to the fourth. When the fourth house or that lord are activated by a predictive technique, we should expect either travel or miscommunication or misunderstandings in the native's relationship to his or her family.

What I recommend is that you look at your own natal chart: go through each planet in turn, and write down which of its signs (if any) it is in aversion to, and think about that area of life—especially in the context of a timing device like profections. You should find themes of non-communication, misunderstanding, travel, ignorance, acting impulsively and without information, or events which catch someone unawares.

Exercise: Look at the following chart and answer the questions below. The chart uses whole sign houses.[30]

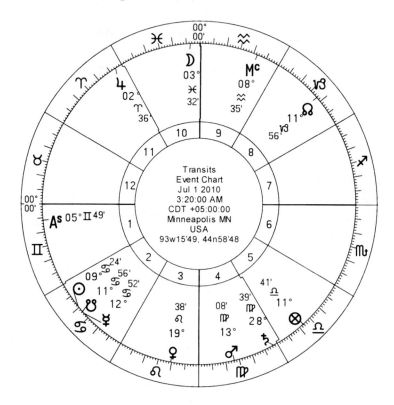

1. Is Venus in aversion to any of her domiciles? If so, which one(s)?
2. Does the Moon regard Jupiter by sign?
3. Mars is in aversion to one of his domiciles: which is it?
4. Use the table of orbs above. Is Mercury within proper orbs for a sextile with Saturn?
5. The Moon opposes Saturn by whole sign. Is she within proper orbs for an degree-based opposition with him?

CHAPTER 11: LOTS

Most people have heard of the Lot (or "Part") of Fortune, although there is often very little information on what it means. In traditional astrology you will quickly encounter *many* Lots (insert your joke here about there being "lots" of Lots). Already by the time of Paul of Alexandria in the 4th Century AD, there were over 100 Lots listed in some texts, although it's unlikely that your average astrologer used all or even most of them. For most natal work, you only need about seven or so (depending on what you're interested in). But if you are a mundane or financial astrologer, it might interest you to know that there are Lots for specific commodities: a Lot of beans, for instance, or a Lot of sugar. These Lots were used to predict markets and prices.

But what *is* a Lot? In mechanical terms, it expresses a *proportion*, and interpretively it has to do with concrete outcomes and the flow of events. Let's look first at how to calculate a Lot, especially since the traditional way of reckoning Lots is easier than the modern, algebraic method.

In modern books, Lots are usually expressed in the following way: X - Y + Z, where X and Y and Z indicate specific points in the chart. So for example, we often find that the Lot of Fortune in diurnal charts is calculated as the position of: Moon – Sun + Ascendant. In my own opinion, this is not really a helpful procedure, and it conceals important rationales for why certain Lots were calculated in the way they were. In traditional astrology, a Lot is determined by taking the interval—in zodiacal order—between two places, and then projecting that same distance from a third point (normally the Ascendant). Let's look first at the Lot of Fortune in the figure below.

This is a diurnal chart, because the Sun is above the horizon. Now, the Lot of Fortune is calculated first using the two luminaries, the Sun and the Moon. Because the chart is diurnal, we begin with the more *diurnal* of the two (the Sun), and count the degrees forward in the zodiac until we reach the Moon. Then, we keep this same interval in mind, and project exactly that many degrees forward from the degree of the Ascendant.

The Sun is at 14° 30' Cancer. If we count forward to the Moon at 26° 37' Virgo, this is a distance of 72° 07'. Now we take this distance and project it forward from the degree of the Ascendant, which is at 26° 17 Scorpio. This brings us to 08° 25' Aquarius.

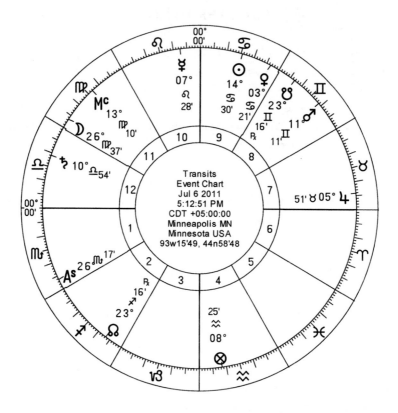

If this had been a nocturnal chart, we would turn the formula around. Instead of starting with the Sun, we would count forward from the more *nocturnal* of the two (the Moon) forward to the Sun, and project those degrees from the Ascendant.

In this way of looking at things, we don't need to remember pluses and minuses, but we simply remember which planets are involved, and which one to start with, based on whether the chart is diurnal or nocturnal. We are always moving forward in the zodiac. I find this much easier and more natural than remembering pluses and minuses.

Now that you know how to calculate the Lot exactly, let me show you a shortcut. For many purposes, we only need to know what sign a Lot is in, and not its exact degree. So let's calculate the Lot again using just our eyes. If we start from the Sun, we can see that the Moon is just beyond his sextile aspect to Virgo. So let's jump to his sextile at 14° Virgo, and we can see that the Moon is about 12° beyond that. This means that the amount we project from the Ascendant will be one sextile, plus about 12°. If we project a sextile from the Ascendant, we reach 26° Capricorn. If we add 12° more, we cross over into early Aquarius at about 8°, which is exactly what we got with the more accurate method. To use this shortcut, you want to be sure that your counting doesn't bring you to within a couple of degrees of a sign boundary. If it does, you should use the more exact method to be sure which sign the Lot falls in.

Let's calculate a different Lot, the Lot of Marriage according to Hermes (I use this in my own practice). This Lot is constructed using Saturn and Venus, which signify stability and ties (Saturn) and romantic love (Venus). Let's suppose this is the chart of a man. For a diurnal male, the Lot is constructed by starting with the diurnal planet (Saturn), and counting forward to Venus, and then projecting that same distance from the Ascendant. But for a nocturnal male, we would start with the nocturnal planet (Venus), and count forward to Saturn, projecting that same distance from the Ascendant. Let's use the shortcut method here. Saturn is at 10° Libra, and we must count forward to Venus at 3° Cancer. You can see that if we cross over to Saturn's opposition at 10° Aries and add two more signs, we get to 10° Gemini. Venus is in the next sign, about 23° away, because there are 20° degrees left in Gemini, and she is 3° beyond that. So, we must go to the opposition of the Ascendant, add two more signs, plus 23°. The opposition of the Ascendant is at 26° Taurus. Adding two more signs gets us to 26° Cancer. Now we have to add 23°. You can easily see that this will put us well into Leo, so for most purposes we could stop here and say that the Lot of Marriage is in Leo. But if we wanted to be a little more exact, we'd say that there are 4° left in Cancer, which leaves 19° to go. The Lot is at about 19° Leo. (It's actually at 18° 44' Leo).

As I mentioned, for many purposes Lots are considered to occupy the whole sign, and not simply a specific degree. So, if a Lot falls on 14° Gemini, then Gemini itself is considered to be the location of the Lot. This is not a matter of laziness or insecurity about mathematics. For instance, when looking at transits, you may have noticed that when a planet enters a certain sign, there is an effect pertaining to that house even though the planet has not yet reached a cusp or other specific point. Likewise, when a planet enters a sign containing a Lot, the Lot may be activated even though the planet has not yet reached the exact degree of the Lot.

One other feature of the Lots is drawn from a specific characteristic of the Lot of Fortune: namely, that the whole-sign angles from Lots (and specifically the Lot of Fortune) are more "energetic."[31] So for example, in the chart above the Lot of Fortune is in Aquarius. This means that natal planets and transits to the whole-sign angles of the Lot of Fortune are more energetic—the sign itself, its two squares, and the opposing sign: Aquarius, Scorpio and Taurus, and Leo.

But what does this really mean? Let's take a look first at what Fortune meant to ancient people. We are used to speaking of both good and bad fortune, but ancient philosophers like Aristotle tried to express what exactly is meant by Fortune. Aristotle's own example[32] is this. Suppose you decide one day to go to the marketplace. While you are looking at vegetables and spices and chickens, you suddenly bump into a man who owes you money, and he pays you that money. Aristotle wants to know the following: what has caused this to happen, and is Fortune itself a cause of events?

What you have to understand is that this example comes from Aristotle's *Physics*, which has in part to do with what causes events and change. We know that normal, everyday elements and forces cause certain things to happen, but most people would also call this accidental payment of money a matter of "good fortune." So, what is Fortune exactly, and how is it a cause? Aristotle says that Fortune does cause things, but in a very special way. It has the following features:

- It can't be something that always or usually happens (for those things happen by necessity through normal, natural causes).
- It must serve a purpose, i.e., for our benefit or harm.
- Although it is related to choice, the situation you are presented with was not initiated because of your choice.
- It is physically caused by indefinitely many normal, everyday causes.

So it's not like you were physically forced to go to the market or are there all the time; being paid was related to choices in your life, but you didn't make an explicit decision to find the man; it served conventionally good or bad purposes or effects (having money is good!); and it was the result of indefinitely many other normal causes: you went to the market because you were out of food, he came to the market because it was a nice day and his mother needed medicine, and he had just gotten his paycheck, and because

---

[31] Valens, *Anthology* IV.7.
[32] *Physics* II.4.

the market was crowded at one end he made his way to your end, and so on...

Astrologically, what this means is roughly the following: the place of the Lot of Fortune indicates how and whether (and when) the native will be within the flow of events, so as to reap conventionally good and bad things, being able to take advantage of (or suffer) things she has not herself chosen, but which present themselves to her. Since the whole-sign angles of the Lot are also energetic, then planets and transits and other predictive methods that take place in those places, will also be rather energetic and partake of this flow of events.

One way to look at this is in terms of some traditional statements about a person's social status and eminence. Traditional astrologers created a kind of hierarchy of conditions to describe levels of ease and success in life, from those who enjoy the greatest fortune and eminence (and without much effort), to those who suffer lots of bad luck and need to struggle to make ends meet. One of the indications for a poorer life, is having the Lot of Fortune in the twelfth house. Now, why is that?

Well, we can look at this statement in two ways. First of all, if the Lot of Fortune is in the twelfth, then it is in aversion to the Ascendant: it is as though the flow of events and opportunities is not really available to the native, or the native is rarely in the right place at the right time, or even doesn't recognize the opportunities. On the other hand, it means that the flow of events is focused on the twelfth house (mistakes, enemies), so again the types of opportunities and events that the native does find herself in, may not be very helpful.

Does this mean that the native cannot be successful at all in life? No. It is true that about 1/12 of humanity will have the Lot of Fortune in the twelfth, and probably at least 1/12 of humanity does struggle and labor. But it could also mean this: someone with such a Lot of Fortune has to *make her own luck*: while many conventionally negative things might be present in life, the native has to work hard to succeed, because good things are not presented to her on a silver platter. So she could still be successful, but it might require much more personal effort to overcome obstacles. This is a way of distinguishing what seems merely fated (having the Lot in the twelfth) from the native's *reaction* to life: that is, the need to work hard to make her own luck. Not everyone undertakes such effort, and the sad fact is that many people will fail even with effort. But as practicing astrologers, we can point out the need for such work, and the presence of this bad luck (or the difficulty of being in the right place at the right time), and help our clients deal realistically with that. Sometimes we are well-placed in the flow of events, sometimes not, and that's the truth about life.

The Lots and their whole-sign angles are used in predictive methods, too. Without getting into specifics about techniques, when a timing technique involves one of these whole-sign angles especially, we often see a notable event pertaining to a given Lot.

CHAPTER 12: TWO RULES FOR INTERPRETING CHARTS

I once gave a talk to a group of modern astrologers, and was teaching a certain medieval technique that involved finding the Lot of Fortune. But in the back of the room I noticed a young woman who was visibly very upset. It turned out that she had only been studying astrology for a couple of months, and felt very lost. I went over and asked if she had a copy of her birth chart. She had a copy that had been printed out by someone else, and it looked something like this:

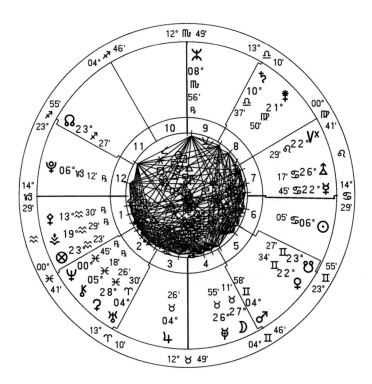

I told her to put her chart away and just try to follow the method in her head.

This chapter is not really about how our charts look (though I think people should use simpler diagrams), but it serves as a good metaphor for what I want to express. As astrologers we are visual people. We like to look at charts. But in a chart like the one above, we can easily get thrown by all of the symbols and lines and details: our eyes move to one thing, and then we are easily led to another, and another, and pretty soon we are lost. For many people, when trying to understand something about the client, the same thing happens: we look at Venus, then we suddenly see an aspect, then we jump to another planet, look at its sign, see something else, and so on. Pretty soon it seems as though everything in the whole chart is implicated in one simple issue. This jumbling of symbols and in our approach can affect our eyes and our minds, and lead to confusion.

One benefit of traditional astrology is the use of rules and methods. Rules do not prevent counseling or hinder us from helping a client understand what something means in their lives. They are not there to restrict us in some bad Saturnian fashion. Rather, they *enhance* our ability to help: *traditional astrology helps us block out the noise, so that we know how to proceed, and not get overwhelmed.*

Traditional texts usually proceed by defining a problem, identifying what to look at, and then listing a variety of possibilities—often going from the easiest and most obvious things to note, to some more obscure and second-best indications for what you seek. The goal of this kind of approach is to help you *rank and prioritize what you are looking for.* Even if everything in the chart is somehow implicated in some situation with your marriage or your brother, most indicators offer so little information, or are so tangential, that they can often be safely ignored. Traditional astrology helps you *slow down* and *discipline your mind* so that you don't end up feeling confused and throw out a bunch of intuitive guesses as to what something means.

Let me first outline a few things about what traditional astrologers generally think a planet does,[33] then I'll give you two key rules for interpreting *any chart.* In general, every planet does four things simultaneously, and you should think of them in this order when you interpret what a planet means:

- **Natural or general signification**. This means nothing more than that each planet tries to be itself, indicating something of its nature in the most general way. Some natural or general significations of Venus are: love, partying, play, beauty, jewelry, a sister, and so on. We are all familiar with this. What we must add to this basic nature is the planet's condition, such as moving direct or retrograde, being in its detriment or domicile, and so on. The planetary condition

---

[33] I am drawing on explicit teachings from Robert Zoller and Morin here, but they are generally applicable to all traditional texts.

identifies something of the quality of the planet's natural or general indications.

- **Location**. Each planet tries to be itself, but in a way that is focused on a particular house. So if Venus is in the eleventh, she indicates Venusian friends; in the seventh, a Venusian partner or interpersonal relationships. Again, this will be modified by the planetary condition.

- **Rulership**. Each planet is trying to be itself, in a certain condition, in a certain house, but so that it also manages the houses it rules. If a planet is in the eleventh but rules the ninth, then it is managing ninth-house matters (spirituality, travel, and so on) by means of the house it is in (friendships), using its own style (natural signification), and according to the condition it is in.

- **Aspects**. It might come as a surprise, but generally speaking aspects are the last things traditional astrologers examine. Aspects are like a kind of partnership, but we need to know *who* the partners are and what they want, before we can describe how their partnership will work out. Mercury in a sextile to Mars may be characterized to some extent on its own, but we will not have a complete understanding of this aspect unless we know what Mercury and Mars mean, their conditions, where they are focusing their energy, and what areas of life they are managing.

From here we can move to two basic rules of delineation:

Rule #1: Location is more immediate than rulership. I get this rule from my teacher Robert Zoller, and the 17th Century astrologer Morin. But normally it's stated as though location is "stronger" than rulership. I don't quite agree with this, because one fault of traditional astrologers is that they often overuse terms like "strength" and "weakness." The point of this rule is to say that (a) a planet acts most immediately and directly through the house it is in, and (b) when looking at a house, planets in it will be the more immediate influences on that house, as opposed to what the lord of the house indicates. Let's look right away at a chart:

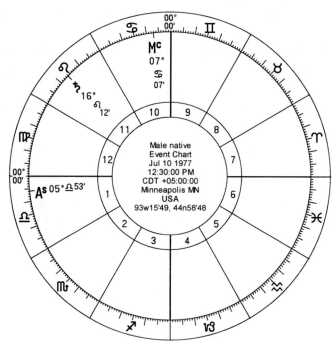

This is based on a nativity we'll look at in Chapters 13 and 14, but I've simplified it so we can concentrate on just one thing. In the chart, Libra is rising, and so by whole signs all of Libra is the first house. Saturn is in Leo, the eleventh house. Saturn also rules the fourth (Capricorn) and the fifth (Aquarius). So Saturn is first of all being himself, then he is himself in the eleventh, and then he rules two other houses through the eleventh. So let's ask, "What is Saturn doing in this chart?" The most immediate thing he is doing is eleventh-house things. (It helps to think about it abstractly like this at first, so you don't get too carried away with interpretive possibilities.) The eleventh house means friends and friendships. So of all the areas of life, Saturn is most immediately affecting friendships. Another way to say this is that he signifies Saturnian friends or friendship experiences.

On the other hand, let's ask ourselves, "What is going on with this person's eleventh house?" The eleventh house is Leo, which is ruled by the Sun. But because Saturn is there, Saturn has the most immediate effect for eleventh-house matters. The Sun will be doing something for the friendships too, but his effect is not as immediate as Saturn's. So Saturn's own immediate effect is on the eleventh, and the most immediate effect on the eleventh is Saturn's presence there.

Well, what can we say about this? If we think generally about what a Saturnian friend would be like, we'd say, "older, conservative, authoritative, long-lasting, limiting," and that sort of thing. But note that he is in Leo. You learned in Chapter 8 that Saturn is in his detriment in Leo, and planets in detriment show disintegration and corruption. So although the chart shows Saturnian friends, it shows Saturnian friends with disintegration and corruption. Traditionally, a Saturn like this shows dishonest, criminal friends, or (just because of the detriment) friendships that fall apart and disintegrate.

In fact, one theme of this native's life is that he has often had unreliable friends, low-class friends, and friendships that are unstable (or involve unstable people) and fall apart. This is a general theme in his life, and because it is his natal chart, he will always have this theme. But as with any chart, we cannot make this information really practical until we apply a predictive technique to see *when* this Saturn is activated. As we'll see in Chapter 13, profections are a handy way to tell when a planet is activated. Saturn will not only be activated according to his location, but also according to the houses he rules. This brings us to the second rule.

Rule #2: What is indicated by a house, emanates from the lord of that house. This rule is an extension of what I've said about the lord of a house having management responsibility over that house. Basically, it means that the lord of a house will try to bring about and effect whatever that house means, through the house it is actually in, in conjunction with the various planetary conditions it is in and aspects it makes. Let's jump right to an example, and see how this is combined with the previous rule.

This chart has Scorpio rising, with the Moon in the seventh whole-sign house and Venus in the third. Now, look at the ninth house: it is Cancer. The ninth house signifies foreigners, higher education, travel, spirituality, and so on. Let's ask, "What is going on with this person's ninth house? How are travel, foreigners, and so on, manifesting in her chart?" Our first rule says that location is more immediate than rulership, so we should first see if there are any planets actually in the ninth: in this modified chart, there are none. So, we move to our second rule, which says that what is signified by a house, emanates from the lord of that house. We look to the lord of Cancer (the Moon) to see how these ninth-house things manifest and are brought about. The Moon is in the seventh, which signifies marriage and partnerships (among other things). So we can say that foreigners and spirituality (for example) appear in the form of, and are brought about by, relationships. Somehow the native's relationships will be an important channel through which her experiences of spirituality and foreigners will manifest. A simple way to say this is: "Her primary relationships will be connected to foreigners." Or even, "She will marry a foreigner."

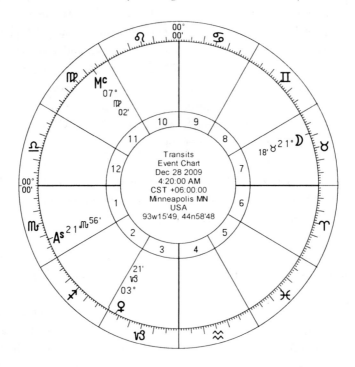

We can even look at it from the other direction. Suppose we look at the seventh house (Taurus) and ask, "With whom will this person get involved or marry?" Since there is a planet in the seventh, this will be a more immediate effect on the seventh than the fact that Venus rules Taurus. An immediate effect upon the relationships will be the presence of spirituality and foreigners, because the Moon, who's in the seventh, rules the ninth and will manifest that ninth through relationships.

What else can we say about this Moon, relationships, and foreigners? Well, in general we may say that the partners will have some Lunar characteristics, they will be Lunar-type people. The Moon is exalted, and we learned in Chapter 8 what that means: a refined, elegant, confident and respected person, or at least these kinds of experiences.

Notice that we have been able to say all of this without even looking at Venus, who rules the seventh. Actually, because the Moon is the exalted lord of the Taurus, I would probably not pay much attention to Venus, because since the Moon (as the exalted lord) is actually in the house, she will in a certain sense be taking over for Venus. But if we had to look at Venus for managing the relationships, we'd note that she is in the third (Capricorn). Now, the third house is also a spiritual house in traditional astrology, and so to my mind she further points to spirituality, and perhaps even someone involved in nature religions or who values the earth (Capricorn is an earthy sign). Maybe it means meeting the spouse through third-house situations.

Although different kinds of charts have specialized rules (such as in horary, mundane, elections), all charts still have the same basic principles that involve location and rulership. These two simple rules, combined with other things like dignities, will allow you to gain valuable information from *any kind of chart*.

Exercise: Look at the following combinations of location and rulerships, and see if you can state what they might mean. Don't worry about what planets might be involved, or their condition.[34]

1. The lord of the second is in the eleventh. What does this tell you about the native's financial situation?
2. The lord of the tenth is in the sixth. What does this tell you about the native's professional life and reputation?
3. The lord of the Ascendant is in the fifth. What does this tell you about the native's sense of purpose and her interests?

---

[34] For answers, see Appendix C.

CHAPTER 13: PREDICTIVE TECHNIQUES

Without thinking, quickly name an obvious predictive technique in modern astrology. You probably thought: "transits." Traditional astrologers use transits too, but in a different way. The main differences here between modern and traditional astrology are (1) the use of "time lords," and (2) the prioritizing of predictive techniques. Transits provide a good way of understanding these differences.

You've probably had the experience of looking for very nice transits to your natal chart: let's say, a lovely Venus-Jupiter transit. Maybe you saw in your ephemeris when this transit would happen, and you were very excited: maybe you even noted the time of the exact transit, and waited for good things to emerge at that moment—and then nothing at all happened! You might have wondered why you didn't have the great experience you expected. In traditional astrology, there are ways of explaining why nothing happened.

The first thing to understand is the idea of a "time lord." Unlike a transit, which usually denotes events over a very short period of time, several traditional techniques assign one or more planets to govern your life (or some area of life) for longer periods of time: these planets are called time lords. For example, in the method called "profections" (see below), one planet rules your life for an entire year, from birthday to birthday. In the method called "distributions," two planets cooperate in ruling your life for periods that might last up to 12 years or so. It's like looking to the President or the Prime Minister when asking what a country as a whole is doing: since that political figure is in charge of the nation, what he or she does is extremely important for understanding the direction of the nation. Just so, these time lords set themes for your life during these periods, though of course they are not going to dictate events every day. If Mars is your time lord, you are not going to have a Martial event every second of every day, but Mars will establish a theme that will be particularly activated during his rulership.

What activates a time lord? Often, it is a transit of or to that time lord. That is, whereas in modern astrology transits are often the *first* thing people look at, in traditional astrology transits are normally the *last* think we look at. First we need to identify the time lords, and *then* identify transits involving them. So if you were waiting for your Venus-Jupiter transit and nothing happened, it is likely that *neither of those planets was a time lord* during that period. Transits are like activating influences, but they often only activate what was already indicated by a time lord!

Following is a list of common traditional predictive methods:[35]

- **Distribution**. This involves directing a point (like the Ascendant) or planet through the bounds, and judging such periods based on the lord of the bound and any planetary ray or body encountered in it.
- *Firdārīyyāt*. This is a time-lord system that assigns periods of years to each of the seven planets and the Nodes, with further subperiods assigned to the seven planets.
- **Profections**. This advances a point by one sign (or house or 30° increment) per year, looking especially at the planet ruling the place one arrives at. See below.
- **Primary directions**. This moves a planet or point through the zodiac, but based on degrees of the celestial equator rather than simple zodiacal degrees.[36]
- **Solar revolutions**. Also called solar "returns." Traditionally, solar revolution charts are never examined in isolation, but always in relation to the natal chart. Older authors especially treat the solar revolution as a set of transits to the nativity.
- **Transits**. You know what these are! But they are usually coordinated with other time lords, such as the profected lord of the year (see below).

Example: Profections

Astrologers often speak about life moving in cycles. Profection is a central, powerful, and easy-to-understand predictive technique that involves a cyclical view of the chart.

The word "profection" simply means "advancement." The basic idea is simply this: we pick a point in the chart that means something, and advance it by one sign per year from birth, and track what houses and planets we encounter along the way. Most traditional authors say that we can advance anything we like (such as the Sun for profession and recognition), but here I

---

[35] For descriptions of most of these, see *Persian Nativities* III (Appendix A).
[36] See especially Martin Gansten's book in Appendix A.

will advance the Ascendant, which indicates life generally. You should start to use this in your practice immediately!

Historically, there have been three ways to profect something:

- By whole sign. This is the method I use, and it is the oldest way.
- By 30° increments. This is described by 'Umar al-Tabarī.[37]
- By house cusps. This was used especially by later astrologers.

Take a look at the following diagram, which assumes we are profecting from the Ascendant (although the sequence of ages is the same no matter where we begin).

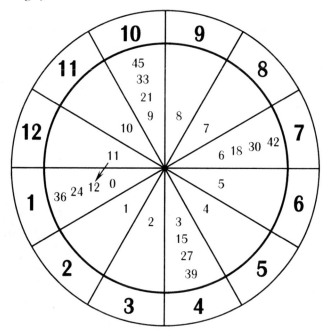

Figure 17: Profection ages from the Ascendant

The inner ring of numbers (from 0 onwards) marks the age of the native. So at birth, the native is 0 years old, and the Ascendant is (so to speak) on itself. When the native has her first birthday and is 1 year old, the profection advances to the second house. When the native is 2 years old, we advance to the third house. If you follow the course of the numbers around the circle, you see that we reach the twelfth house at age 11, and then the profection

---

[37] See *Persian Nativities* II, in Appendix A.

returns to the Ascendant at age 12. The profections continue around and around until the native's death. I have added further ages in the angles so you may see at a glance where the profection arrives every few years. For example, the profection reaches the tenth house at age 45, which means that it will reach the eleventh house at age 46, the twelfth at 47, and the Ascendant at age 48. If we had wanted to profect the seventh to track the native's relationships, we would have started with the seventh house at age 0, the eighth at age 1, and so on. No matter where you begin, the profection will always return to itself at ages 12, 24, 36, 48, *et cetera*, and will always reach its opposite at ages 6, 18, 30, 42, and on and on.

Let's take a look at the following chart, and I'll explain each way of assigning the years, depending on your house system:

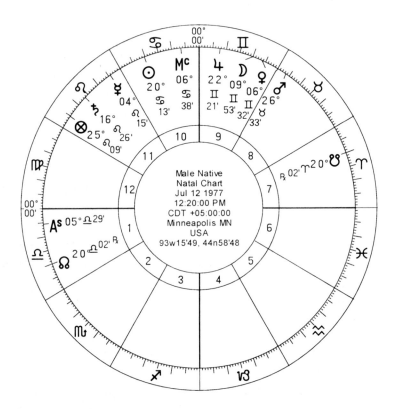

In this chart, Libra is rising. Let's profect the Ascendant, which is the most common method. At birth or age 0, the Ascendant—which indicates life generally—is Libra. But at age 1, the Ascendant advances to the second house, which is Scorpio. At age 2, the Ascendant advances to the third house, which is Sagittarius; and so on. For each year, we advance by one sign, until we reach age 12, which returns to Libra. The cycle continues around and around in increments of twelve, until the native dies. So, the Ascendant (or anything we profect) will return to Libra at ages 12, 24, 36, 48, and so on.

Now, when we reach each house, the lord of that house is called the "lord of the year." This is a time lord, as I mentioned above. It is as though the ruler of that house is responsible for the themes of that year, and you have already learned about rulership in previous chapters. So, at age 18, the profection in this chart reaches Aries, which makes Mars the lord of the year. We have to look at what house we have reached, as well as natal planets in that house, and where the lord of the year is: according to the rules I will explain below, the natal location of the lord of the year will give further information as to what is going on in that year, and what areas of life are brought to bear on it.

In this example, profect the Ascendant to age 30: we will reach the seventh house (Aries), just as at age 18. This means that we might expect seventh-house issues to be of importance, and again Mars is the lord of the year. So in general, the year will proceed according to the nature and activities of Mars and whatever else he is doing in the chart. The seventh house indicates partnerships, controversies, and so on, and Mars is in the eighth, in detriment. The fact that he is in aversion to the seventh means that there is something unsteady or even unconscious or unwitting about what the native is doing, and his detriment means that his plans are disorganized or erratic or will not come to full fruition. In this year, the native was working very hard to have a relationship, but he made missteps because he was trying too hard, and only realized too late that he was undermining himself.

If we profect the Ascendant to age 20, we come to the ninth house (Gemini). So, we might expect travel in that year. I would especially expect this, because one of the planets in that ninth house is Venus, who rules his Ascendant: that is, he himself will take the initiative in bringing ninth-house matters about. The native was moving around the country and even abroad throughout the year. Another planet in the ninth is Jupiter, who rules this sixth. This means that sixth-house matters and people are brought to bear, and he was involved with many lowbrow and socially low people in that year. The lord of the year is Mercury because he rules Gemini, and Mercury is in the eleventh. Not only were his friendships a motive for traveling, but he made a number of friends on his travels.

If we profect the Ascendant to the eleventh house (ages 22, 34, and so on), the profection arrives at Saturn. During that year the native had some problems with dishonest friends and friendships that fell apart. Likewise, when we profect the Ascendant to the houses that Saturn rules (the fourth, the fifth), we also activate Saturn. Because Saturn rules these houses and is in detriment, he showed disintegration and problems with family (the fourth) and in the experience of pleasures and partying (the fifth). In fact, at age 22 the problems not only involved friendships, but they had to do with friendships that were connected with the fourth and fifth houses, because Saturn's rulership of those places drew family, home, and pleasures into the situation.

If you follow the other two profection methods, you may get different results. For instance, according to whole signs, the tenth house is Cancer, and so a profection of the Ascendant to the tenth by whole signs will only include Cancer and any planets in it (the Sun). But if you follow 'Umar's 30° method, the profections will span exactly 30°, from 5° 29' of one sign to 5° 29' to the next sign. So, a profection to the tenth will span from exactly 5° 29' Cancer to exactly 5° 29' Leo. But in the chart you can see that Mercury is at 4° 15' Leo, which is enclosed in that space. So Mercury will be one of the planets to examine that year because he falls within 'Umar's profection. But this will not be so according to whole signs.

The same kind of difference will appear if we used quadrant-based houses, because instead of using whole signs or 30° increments, we will be counting cusps and whatever planets are enclosed between those cusps. This will also involve an irregularity in the order of lords of the year, because if two cusps fall on the same sign, then the same planet will be the lord of the year for two years in a row. And if a sign is intercepted between cusps, then the lord of the intercepted sign will never be the lord of the year at the relevant age.

Whichever method you use, one advantage of profections is that you do not need an ephemeris to understand them: your natal chart alone sets the themes for each year.[38] Moreover, since profections always return to themselves every twelve years, you can always think back twelve years to get a hint of what the current year has in store for you.

---

[38] To do a full treatment, you'd want to look at your solar revolution, which is discussed in my *Persian Nativities III* and in downloadable lecture from my site (www.bendykes.com).

CHAPTER 14: A SHORT CASE STUDY

Let's apply a little of what we've learned to the chart we examined in the previous chapter. I'm not going to go through everything in this chart, but let's look at some of the basics by focusing on the chart as a whole, and especially the Ascendant and its lord.

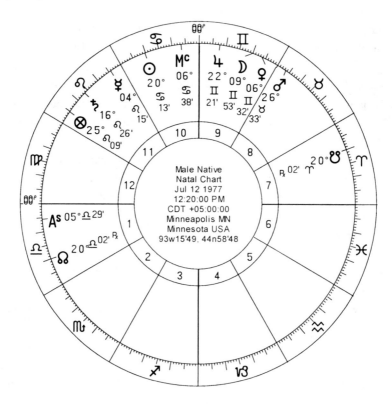

First, let's take a look at the chart as a whole: what kinds of planets and signs are emphasized? Both of the benefics are in the ninth, which is an advantageous place for the native, but dynamically they are cadent and weak. Both of them are also peregrine and in common signs, which suggests restlessness and a sense of being out of place, as well as a dependence on their domicile lord (Mercury) for their operation. Both of the malefics are of medium dynamical strength, but Mars is in a place that is not advantageous for the native, and is in detriment. Saturn is in the eleventh and in detriment,

which (as we saw before) has ill effects upon friendships and hopes. The only angular planet is the Sun in the tenth, also peregrine.

Of the signs, the degrees of the angles are on movable signs, with the lord of the Ascendant (which represents the native) in a common sign. The Moon is also in a common sign, and the Sun is in a movable sign. The preponderance of the life force here is in movable and common signs.

So the first thing we might say about this chart is that there is a lot of change and shifting about in the native's life: the native wants to keep moving, and movable signs in particular will sometimes provoke events so as to move forward. But the strong emphasis on the common signs (with no planet having a dignity) also suggests uncertainty. If the planets had been in their own domiciles or exaltations, this would have suggested self-possession and confidence. The cadence of the benefics and succeedent character of the malefics, warns us that—on the whole—conventional goods will be less accessible and more fleeting, whereas conventional evils will tend to be more prominent (note that both of the malefics are in fixed signs, which signify something lasting). But do remember that benefic planets are still benefics: even though they may be peregrine and cadent, they still provide conventionally good things. So despite their problems, the ninth house (where they are located) will be a source of good things and pleasure for the native, even if mixed with problems.

But this is just a general picture of the chart. To go deeper, we need to start looking at locations and rulerships and aspects. If we start with the Ascendant, we see it is Libra. Libra is a movable, airy sign, ruled by Venus. It is a rather social sign, and because it is movable it does not want to stay still and hang around—it wants to initiate, go for things, and even move on quickly from one thing to the next. Because it is ruled by Venus, her sociability is added here, too. For this native, the ability to express this energy will be important for feeling fulfilled and as though things are on track.

The lord of the Ascendant is Venus. Because she manages the Ascendant, the meaning of the native's life and its ability to be expressed will have to be channeled through her: by condition, location, aspects, and so on. Venus is normally a happy planet, sociable, artistic or aesthetic. So the native will try to channel his Libran needs through Venusian experiences and people. And where is she? In the ninth: so ninth-house matters will be a default area in which the native will try to meet his Libran and Venusian needs: travel and foreigners, education and religion, law, and so on. I do notice that two planets in the ninth are also aspecting the degree of the Ascendant within a couple of degrees: Venus and the Moon. This means that Venusian, Lunar, and ninth-house energies are especially important for, and accessible to, the native.

Let's look a little more closely at Venus. She is within a couple of degrees from the Moon, who rules the tenth house. That is, the native's sense of himself (Venus) is in close contact with his professional goals and need to be recognized. Do you see that Sun in the tenth? That's often an indication of wanting to be in the view of the public somehow (whether in government, television, entertainment, or simply being renowned). The fact that the Moon, who is the lord of the tenth, so closely aspects the degree of the Ascendant and is with the lord of the Ascendant, is a classic sign of finding this kind of public recognition. But the Moon is also in aversion to the tenth (signifying unsteadiness and breaks), and there is that problem of being peregrine. Luckily, both the Moon and Venus are in a (separating) reception by Mercury, so he adds some stability. Because Mercury is in the eleventh, his most immediate effect will be to signify friends: and so we might say that friends are of some aid to the native in achieving his need for aesthetic outlets and public recognition.

Speaking of Mercury: although he is in the eleventh (friends), he rules the ninth. Just as we did in an earlier chapter, we can ask: what kinds of friends does he indicate? Mercurial friends to be sure, but also foreign friends (the ninth). So we might especially expect the role of foreign friends to be prominent in this native's life purpose.

Notice that we've been able to get something of a good overview of this native's life, just by focusing on the general features of the chart, and the Ascendant and its lord. We have identified both some of the things that he wants and what his general energy style is, as well as having identified some potential problems to discuss with him. Nor have we used his Sun sign to describe him as "a Cancer."

This native is a part-time professional singer. He is sociable, loves to meet new people and be on the stage, and has an irresistible urge to travel, whereby he also meets many new friends and contacts that he is able to draw on later. But as I mentioned in the previous chapter, there are also some issues with instability in his friendships, and when he does travel some of the people he meets are unreliable, or he encounters unusual mishaps. This was due to Saturn in detriment in the eleventh, and Jupiter in detriment in the ninth, ruling the sixth. These themes are not always active and up-front, but are especially activated during key profections.

When this man was 31 years old, he came to me for some advice. He wanted to move out of the country for an extended period. At age 31, his Ascendant was profected to the eighth house, which as you can see has Mars in detriment in it. Does this look like a favorable time to make serious changes in life? Not really. Simply by being in the sign of the year, Mars will bring his energy to bear, and his energy is not too helpful. Mars can show travel because he shows severing and disconnections, but he is in detriment in the eighth, indicating fear and trouble and possible money problems (he rules the native's second house, and the eighth is also a house of debt). Because this sign is Taurus, it means that Venus is the lord of the year. She is in the ninth, and is also the lord of the Ascendant. Since she is in the ninth, it is a further indication that he would probably travel anyway, and because she rules the Ascendant, it suggests that these plans to travel were closely tied to his sense of purpose in life. So, I wasn't sure whether my advice would matter.

I suggested to him that he wait a year to travel, when his profection would reach the ninth itself, with both of the benefics in it. But by that time he had already committed himself to the trip, though he had not yet bought the tickets. I asked him, "Why don't you wait for a year to be more financially stable? It seems like there's something hasty about this decision." Indeed, he himself had trouble explaining why he had decided to move out of the country. But he said something to me that made a lot of sense, based on what we have seen so far: "I feel as though there is adventure out there, and that if I don't take advantage of it right now, I'm afraid I'll miss out on it." This is a good example of what we saw with the movable and common signs, and the ninth-house emphasis. He was restless and was determined to make a dramatic move, but he was also feeling insecure and hesitant.

In the end, he moved ahead with his plans. Although he did get singing jobs and was having a lot of fun, within a few months he hit a streak of bad luck and was running out of money. He ended up doing hard labor on a farm and felt lost, not sure what he was going to do next. This aptly describes the eighth-house profection, as well as the beginning of the ninth-house profection at age 32—remember that Jupiter in detriment, ruling the sixth (labor, suffering). He returned to the United States in the ninth-house profection, but this turned out to have some advantages. Because once the profection reached the ninth, with that Venus and Moon (the lord of the tenth) in it, he suddenly got some opportunities to sing and perform in his own city, and his career seemed to take off.

This example not only shows how a few simple rules and concepts can give much concrete information, but it also gives some insight into counseling. Although most of the chart is not the native's mind, the native's mind is also described well in it. The choice to travel was up to him, but his statements and the chart description also show that he was unlikely to listen to my advice anyway—during that year, at least. Should I have advised him to wait? As an astrologer, yes. But I knew it might not make a difference. What if he had followed my advice? Surely something else would have happened that is indicated by Mars and the lord of the year, but it wouldn't have happened in the same way. Maybe from a God's-eye perspective he was fated to travel that year and experience everything he did. But astrologers are not God, we can only read the indications. Clients can only make their own decisions, based on their character and their own view of their circumstances.

CHAPTER 15: FREQUENTLY ASKED QUESTIONS

In this chapter I'd like to respond to some questions and challenges often posed about traditional astrology. Although I answer each one as best I can, we must understand that these challenges often come from different *philosophical positions*: it's not just a technical question of whether something works in a chart or not, or whether outer planets are important, and so on. You will also notice that many of the challenges and questions overlap. I think this is because there are really only a few core areas of dispute, especially the following: moral categories like good and bad, the relation between prediction and choice (i.e., determinism), and whether traditional astrology is chart-centered rather than being client-centered. I have already addressed these issues to a great extent in previous chapters, but it's worth reviewing them again here in a more sustained way.

1. Traditional astrology dwells on the negative and the bad.

First, let's distinguish issues of good and bad from issues of fate and choice. Good and bad are values that pertain to both fate-based and freedom-based philosophies. I may be fated to do something good or bad, or I might have the freedom to choose something good or bad. Values are not the same as the metaphysics of fate or freedom. I'll discuss issues of fate, freedom and choice itself in a bit.

Traditional astrology itself doesn't really dwell on the negative, it is just more realistic about how mixed life is. Almost nothing in life is unconditionally good or bad. Getting married can be a good, but so is having a career: if getting married and having kids means giving up your career, isn't that a mixture of good and bad? People notice what is bad more readily because we feel it more strongly. But how often do we really count our blessings and recognize the things that have gone really well? This is a problem for humanity, not for traditional astrology.

But sometimes people think that traditional *texts* dwell on the bad. Actually, traditional texts routinely give both the best, worst, and middling interpretations of various planetary placements: this allows the astrologer to get a sense of the range of possibilities, depending on what the planets are doing. Identifying real problems is also the morally responsible thing to do, because if we are trying to help people solve their problems, we must first recognize that there is a problem. I once heard an astrologer say about older astrology books, "anytime you read something negative…put it out of your head." Unfortunately, this really epitomizes a widespread modern belief that *you can always be successful, and only have good experiences, and do anything you want, simply if you want to.* Or, that *you can create your own reality.* This is an unrealistic and irresponsible attitude that leads to bad advice.

The strange thing is that many modern astrologers themselves often dwell on the negative. This is partly due to our human fascination with the bad and the macabre. But if you think about it, moderns have essentially introduced three new malefic planets: Uranus, Neptune, and Pluto. Even though many people say that Neptune can mean exalted spirituality, Uranus the breaking down of unhelpful structures, and Pluto transformation, I have never or hardly ever seen modern astrologers scour the chart for these things in their strictly positive sense. When many modern astrologers look at a chart, the *first* thing they usually do is look at the outer planets to find delusion (Neptune), destruction and the bizarre (Uranus), and violence and abuse (Pluto). We might even say that modern astrology uses these three planets and their malefic qualities (and excessively so) as a springboard for introducing ideas of evolution, spirituality, and potentials. In a certain sense, modern astrology at its core *needs* these planets to act as malefics.

2. A focus on events rather than client potentials

"Traditional astrologers are overly concerned with predicting concrete events, as though people do not have choices: why don't you focus on potentials instead?"

Actually, traditional astrology deals with a lot of potentials. In part this simply means that it is up to you to decide how to manage your life, given various things that may be predicted in the chart. It also has to do with what I call a "determinism of types," which I'll describe in questions 3 and 4 below. But first, let me talk about potentials generally.

The word "potential" simply means the "power" or ability to do something, or for something to happen. But there is a big difference between a mere possibility and a meaningful potential. For example, I might become the Queen of England. That is what I would call a "mere possibility." It is not a very meaningful potential, since to become *actual*, it would demand large-scale changes in English law, a sex-change operation, plus a million other things. If my chart shows various signs of royalty or high office, would it be right for an astrologer to tell me that being the Queen of England is in my potential? No. Speaking about pure potentials in and of themselves is not very informative, because in the abstract they are not much different from mere dreaming and wishful thinking.

Something potential is really only meaningful when we link it to conditions that make it *actual*. If your son's teacher tells you he is not living up to his potential, this means that his character and surroundings are ripe for him to actualize his skills, not that just anything at all is possible. In real life, our being and nature is defined more by what we *actually* do and what is realistically in our power to do. This includes failure: if we can and should do something, but through our own choices we fail to do it, that fact also describes us. So we need to recognize real potentials, but mere possibilities that cannot come to pass or are extremely unlikely to do so, are more or less idle.

In traditional astrology, we are highly attuned to potentials that can be actualized—this is especially true in electional astrology. It means focusing on potentials which the native can and most likely will choose, based on his or her circumstances or character—all of which is well defined by the chart or in consultation with the client. The same is true in modern astrology: a person of such-and-such a character does have the mere possibility of doing all sorts of things, and maybe through persuasion and consulting with an astrologer the client may rise to the occasion. But there is a contradiction between seeing what a person's character is, and claiming that he or she equally has the potential to do all sorts of things contrary to that character.

Finally, we should recognize that modern approaches to potentials usually assume only potentials that relate to conventional goods (rather than evils): becoming more spiritual and wise, wealthy, having better relationships. But people also have real potentials for evil. We may not be able to stop a Hitler from actualizing his potential, but does that mean we should encourage him to be Hitler simply because he has the potential to do it? No. We should recognize the importance of potentials, but not assume that simply because it is a potential, it is good to actualize.

3. The stars cannot limit us, you cannot predict behavior.

"Traditional astrology tries to predict behavior, but astrology is a language of interpretive symbols, it cannot say what we will and won't do."

The first thing to say is that *of course* astrologers predict behavior (or look for it retroactively), even modern astrologers. Generally speaking, predicting behavior is something we do all the time, even outside of astrology: parents can often predict the behavior of their children, and people often know how their friends will act. But to understand how this works in astrology, we need to look more closely at what we mean by a symbol, and what it implies about behavior.

Consider a doctor examining a symptom. A symptom is like a symbol, an indication of something. But since many diseases have similar symptoms, not every symptom in isolation will point directly to a specific disease. Instead, a symptom is a *type*: it narrows down a class of possibilities. The doctor does not necessarily see the disease directly, but he sees an indication. The more indications that are present, the more confidently he can identify and predict the course of the disease.

Astrologically we are dealing with much the same thing. Astrological symbols are meaningless unless they identify types which exclude other possibilities. Venus in a particular condition may have a range of meanings and thus of specific behaviors; but Venus is not Saturn or Mercury, so there is still a restriction on the types of behaviors indicated. If a symbol can mean anything, then it means nothing.

In practice, this means we are often indirectly predicting behavior even when we are only trying to interpret topics. For example, suppose a chart indicates marriage, and so the astrologer predicts marriage. But what is that prediction but a claim that the client will get married precisely because she behaves in such a way so as to get married? Or suppose a horary chart predicts getting a new job: that is nothing more than the prediction that the client and the employer will act in such a way as to produce employment. Likewise, even if we have a psychological focus, we indirectly predict behavior because people behave in no other way than according to what impulses and attitudes and value-judgments are in their soul. Every kind of horoscopic astrology predicts behavior.

But this does not mean that every behavior can be predicted down the finest detail. A chart can't show whether I will reach for a sandwich with my right or left hand, nor whether I will comb my hair for thirty seconds or a full minute—those are behaviors which do not make astrological sense. Mundane charts have such a general applicability to huge populations, that trying to predict individuals' exact behaviors is pointless. But in normal cases of marriage, employment, and so on, every type of astrologer ultimately does predict or analyze behavior, and we should simply admit the extent to which we do.

Astrology by itself will not tell us how absolutely determined the world really is: for the most part, in astrology we can only deal with types. The world may in reality be determined more or less, but we should admit that in astrology we at least have a *determinism of types*. Without assuming at least a determinism of types, then chart-reading is useless. If the world were indeterminate, or if people actually exercised radically indeterminate free will on a widespread level, then the natal chart would be irrelevant by the time of adolescence or even earlier.

4. Fate and choice: do traditional astrologers destroy the possibility of meaningful choice?

"Partly because traditional astrologers claim such accuracy and specific results from their predictions, they imply fate and destroy the possibility of meaningful choice. But people do make meaningful choices, so traditional astrologers are wrong to rely on notions of determinism and fate."

The quick answer to this argument is that traditional astrology is indeed compatible with meaningful choice. But in order to explain this, I need to make a couple of distinctions.

First of all, being accurate and specific is not the same thing as believing in universal fate or determinism. Accurate statements are opposed to falseness, and being specific is opposed to being vague: these have to do with issues of truth and detail, not fate. I should hope that astrologers want to help their clients by being both accurate and specific! Otherwise, we have no business claiming to help people understand their life situations. This goes both for interpreting a natal chart, and using predictive techniques.

Second, even fate or determinism is compatible with meaningful choice, provided that we locate the physical and moral meaning of actions in the right place. Many people believe that choice is only meaningful (and carries moral responsibility) if we have the free ability to do otherwise. What most people mean by this is that morality and meaningful choice requires having an absolutely free and indeterminate ability to do something totally different. But this has some strange consequences. For instance, suppose I am sitting next to a man on a train. If I have completely indeterminate free will, then at any moment I am equally capable of killing him and not killing him. But this means that if I do not kill him (which is a good thing), then I am good precisely because although I was equally able of killing him for no reason at all, I did not. The notion that my goodness should depend on *this* sort of alternative action, seems very odd to me, and it does not go with our normal notions of goodness and choice. In real life we tend to praise people more because their *character* is such that they more or less *cannot* do something like kill someone at any moment and for no reason at all. I don't think anyone would praise a courageous soldier because he was *equally* able to scream and flee but did not: instead, we would praise such a soldier for making the choice to do his duty based on his firm and predictable character. That is, his character made it so he was virtually unable to choose to scream and flee.

So here is an alternative. Instead of locating the meaning of choices in the ability to do otherwise, we could say that responsibility lies in the fact that *we*, and only we, choose things based on our character. That is, we are not forced to do something due to external causes, but our character interacts with the world in such a way that the choices come from us and no one else. This is compatible both with looser notions of determinism, and a strict, thorough-going Stoic determinism. We do not have to believe in indeterminate free will for there to be meaningful choices with moral attributes. The world could be largely determined, and because of the characters we develop over time, even our actions are in a larger sense determined—but the actions originate in us, so we are responsible for the fact and meaning of our actions.

No kind of astrology can tell us whether or not the world *in fact* is determined down to the finest detail, in the strong Stoic sense. That is a question for metaphysics and physics. The most we can say from astrology is that we deal with *types* and *kinds* of events and behavior. Suppose for a moment that the strong Stoic view is true: in that case, really the entire state of the world is implicated in our choices, even though the choice itself originates in us. But no astrologer can claim to describe the entire state of the world. Instead, we can only look at types.

When we do predict events and behavior, we are still using types. We assume that for some event to happen, people must behave in such a way as to bring about the event. In some cases, because we do delineate character and personality in a chart, we can feel pretty confident about that person's choices. But we do not always know in a chart who is doing what, and whether events are happening to us, or we are responding to something happening to us, or whether we are originating the choices because of something not seen in the chart. The most we can do as astrologers is use types to identify things that involve choices, but we don't make those choices irrelevant or meaningless just because they form part of a type of event that we can foresee.

Let me give you two examples. Suppose I predict a more or less external event for a client, such as that she has enemies working against her. The client cannot control the existence of the enemies directly, but she can choose to take actions that flush them out or avoid their full fury. I may even be able to tell whether or not she is the kind of person to make this or that choice, but it is still good for me to warn her about them, and it is up to her to make her choice. This is like predicting rain and recommending that someone take an umbrella: some people do, some do not.

On the other hand, suppose I see indications of marriage in a chart at a certain time. I may be able to predict either legal marriage or a marriage-like event. As I mentioned above, I am predicting that marriage will come about precisely because she will act in such a way as to bring it about. There could be many different ways for that to happen, but I am still dealing at the level of types, and my chart cannot necessarily say exactly how she will act, even though she will still get married. But even if I can tell how she will act, she is still the source of that act and responsible for it, because of the character she has.

So, traditional astrology is compatible with a number of views on determinism and choice, in part because astrology deals at the level of types and categories. It may not be compatible with indeterminate free will, but such free will has moral problems of its own anyway. We can make accurate and specific predictions without denying meaningful choice on the part of clients.

5. Isn't modern astrology more appropriate for modern people? Haven't we evolved from older times?

"Astrology reflects the times and evolutionary state of the people who practice it. We have evolved beyond the days when traditional astrology was relevant. But you traditional astrologers keep harping on William Lilly and others; what can these astrologers from 350 or 2,000 years ago teach us?"

It is true that many things are different now, as compared to 330 years ago. Likewise, I cannot practice astrology now in precisely the way that people will 500 years from now. But that is not an argument for the evolution of astrology. People have not really changed, at least in the ways relevant to astrology: such an assumption is part of modern ideology and pride, it is not based in fact. For instance, under what description of "spiritual evolution" can we explain the wholesale massacres of millions by authoritarian states in the 20th Century, often with the cooperation of their citizens? Astrologically speaking, people still have all of the same concerns as they did 2,000 years ago: Will I be happy? Famous? Get married? Have wealth? What guidance we can give them is not the sole province of modern spiritualities. Ancient philosophies of life are just as relevant now as they were in previous times, and I have described two of these in Chapter 5.

There are a lot of false notions about how people in the past behaved and thought. For example, there is a belief that people in the past were basically fearful, and so they craved predictive astrology in order to control their environment and lives. But what traditional astrology actually shows is that we are all part of a complicated cosmos, and we cannot control everything. Much of what we do astrologically is to help people take advantage of good timing, understanding when things come to be, come to fruition, and pass out of being. That is the human condition, then and now. If anything, some types of *modern* astrology are committed to the idea of control, because they claim we are full of endless potentials that allow us to create our own realities—what is that but a form of total control?

History shows that modern astrology is not a development or evolution out of traditional practice. It's not as though modern astrology has made progress because people judiciously decided what worked, made empirical tests, developed better techniques, and so on. Rather, traditional astrology virtually *disappeared*, and modern astrology was *reinvented*. So when we speak about people like Lilly, we are not worshipping them because they lived in the past. Rather, they were active astrologers dealing with the same problems in life we grapple with today. Instead of worshipping the astrological past for its own sake, we are trying to *rediscover* its approaches, so as to help clients with the same issues found in ancient Greece, medieval Persia, Renaissance England, and modern Melbourne. The precise details of people's problems change, and some of the advice might be more attuned to modern life, but the issues in life are the same.

6. Traditional astrology is both too complicated and oversimplified.

"You traditional astrologers have all of these complicated rules, dignities, categories, all of this unhelpful gray—and yet you claim to boil all of this down to black-and-white, yes-or-no answers."

Life is complicated, so it's important to be able to recognize it in our analysis and vocabulary. *If our vocabulary and concepts are not rich enough, we will not interpret a chart and its events accurately.* In traditional astrology we think we have a rich enough vocabulary to recognize life's complications *as well as* to advise a client about what to expect. But if we don't have all of these things like dignities, aversions, benefics and malefics, we will miss a lot. For example, Venus can mean a lot of things. But there is a big difference between being merely charming and being sleazy: if we cannot bring dignities and other things to bear, then we are not far from having to say, "Well, it could mean all sorts of things; I guess it's up to you to choose your own reality." That is not very helpful for someone who is really concerned about a romantic situation.

Life also has concrete events, and things that do and don't happen: either I had a child last year, or I didn't; I either will get the job, or I won't. And these concrete events often go together with the gray in life: if I ask a horary astrology whether I will get hired for a job, I ultimately expect something close to a yes-or-no answer. But much of that answer depends on how accurately the astrology can reflect all of the complications that go with life's situations. The answer might be "No, because the chart shows that someone else will interfere, and the employer will change her mind." The answer might also be "Yes, but you won't like the job." Such answers depend on recognizing complicated factors that lead to concrete guidance and results.

No responsible traditional astrologer would ever look at a chart and say, "The answer is no. Consultation over. Now go away."

EPILOGUE

We've covered a lot of ground in this book, and really we've only been able to scratch the surface of traditional astrology. I hope you feel that you've been able to learn not only some of the basics, but how these ideas can also help you in your own chart reading.

The traditional revival, which was so well begun by many scholars and practicing astrologers, is spreading and will only show more strength and vibrancy in the years to come. You may decide to advance in these studies and identify more with traditional techniques and concepts. But even if you do not, you should be able to see the humanity and usefulness in the labor of so many of our forebears—most of whose names are lost to history. I wish you much success and happiness in your life and love of astrology.

APPENDIX A: WHERE TO GO FROM HERE

Below I have listed many of the most important and currently available English-language works and resources in traditional astrology, but for reasons of space I have not listed them all. In some of the categories below, I have starred works that are especially good for beginners, and I have sometimes added italicized comments after the bibliographical information.

Important for beginners: Reading traditional texts is not like reading modern ones. Many astrologers wanted to have a more literary style, while others assume you know the vocabulary already; yet others have long lists of conditions and possibilities for interpreting something. The most important thing is: *slow down*. Luckily, this book has already prepared you for a lot of things you will encounter in the works below.

History

Campion, Nicholas, *The Great Year* (London: Arkana, 1994)

Campion, Nicholas, *The Dawn of Astrology: A Cultural History of Western Astrology* (London: Continuum Books, 2008)

Campion, Nicholas, *A History of Western Astrology: The Medieval and Modern Worlds* (London: Continuum Books, 2009)

*Holden, James H., *A History of Horoscopic Astrology* (Tempe, AZ: American Federation of Astrologers, Inc., 1996, updated 2006) *This is an excellent guide to people, dates, and works, even up through the modern period.*

Introductions and general concepts

Abū Ma'shar, *Great Introduction to the Science of the Judgments of the Stars*, Benjamin Dykes trans. (Minneapolis: The Cazimi Press, forthcoming)

Avelar, Helena and Luis Ribeiro, *On the Heavenly Spheres: A Treatise on Traditional Astrology* (Tempe, AZ: The American Federation of Astrologers, 2010)

Bonatti, Guido, *Bonatti on Basic Astrology*, trans. and ed. Benjamin N. Dykes (Minneapolis, MN: The Cazimi Press, 2010)

Bonatti, Guido, *The 146 Considerations*, trans. and ed. Benjamin N. Dykes (Minneapolis, MN: The Cazimi Press, 2010)

Dykes, Benjamin trans. and ed., *Introductions to Traditional Astrology: Abu Ma'shar & al-Qabisi* (Minneapolis, MN: The Cazimi Press, 2010) *This is a joint translation of two introductory works, supplemented with many diagrams and commentary by me.*

Ibn Ezra, Abraham, *The Beginning of Wisdom*, trans. Meira Epstein, ed. Robert Hand (Arhat Publications, 1998)

Morin, Jean-Baptiste, trans. Richard S. Baldwin, *Astrologia Gallica Book 21: The Morinus System of Horoscope Interpretation* (Tempe, AZ: American Federation of Astrologers, Inc., 2008) *Excellent for basic instructions on how to delineate planets in and ruling houses, plus much more. Beginners should skip to Section II, Chapter 2.*

Sahl bin Bishr, *The Introduction* and *The Fifty Judgments*, in Dykes, Benjamin trans. and ed., *Works of Sahl & Masha'allah* (Golden Valley, MN: The Cazimi Press, 2008)

Schmidt, Robert H., trans. and ed. *Definitions and Foundations* (Cumberland, MD: The Golden Hind Press, 2009) *More difficult.*

Nativities and natal prediction

Avelar, Helena and Luis Ribeiro, *On the Heavenly Spheres: A Treatise on Traditional Astrology* (Tempe, AZ: The American Federation of Astrologers, 2010)

Bonatti, Guido, *Bonatti on Nativities*, trans. and ed. Benjamin N. Dykes (Minneapolis, MN: The Cazimi Press, 2010)

Dorotheus of Sidon, *Carmen Astrologicum*, trans. David Pingree (Abingdon, MD: The Astrology Center of America, 2005)

Dykes, Benjamin trans. and ed., *Persian Nativities* vols. I-III (Minneapolis, MN: The Cazimi Press, 2009-10) *Beginners should consult Abu 'Ali in Volume I, and 'Umar in Volume II. Volume III is devoted to predictive techniques (solar revolutions, profections, distributions, and more), and has lots of material for both beginners and more advanced students.*

Firmicus Maternus, trans. James Holden, *Mathesis* (Tempe, AZ: The American Federation of Astrologers, 2011)

Gansten, Martin, *Primary Directions: Astrology's Old Master Technique* (England: The Wessex Astrologer, 2009) *The best book I have seen on primary directions. Much of the book is non-mathematical, but it contains extensive equations in the Appendices.*

George, Demetra, *Astrology and the Authentic Self* (Lake Worth, FL: Ibis Press, 2008) *An excellent example of applying traditional techniques in a modern setting.*

Ibn Ezra, Abraham, *The Book of Nativities and Revolutions*, trans. and ed. Meira B. Epstein and Robert Hand (ARHAT Publications, 2008)

Lilly, William, *Christian Astrology* Vol. III, ed. David R. Roell (Abingdon, MD: Astrology Center of America, 2004)

Māshā'allāh *On the Significations of the Planets in a Nativity* and *What the Planets Signify in the Twelve Domiciles of the Circle*, in Dykes, Benjamin trans. and ed., *Works of Sahl & Māshā'allāh* (Golden Valley, MN: The Cazimi Press, 2008)

Ptolemy, Claudius, *Tetrabiblos*, trans. F.E. Robbins (Cambridge, MA: Harvard University Press, 1998)

Rhetorius of Egypt, *Astrological Compendium*, trans. and ed. James H. Holden (Tempe, AZ: American Federation of Astrologers, Inc., 2009)

Horary

*Bonatti, Guido, *Bonatti on Horary*, trans. and ed. Benjamin N. Dykes (Minneapolis, MN: The Cazimi Press, 2010)

*Bonatti, Guido, *The 146 Considerations*, trans. and ed. Benjamin N. Dykes (Minneapolis, MN: The Cazimi Press, 2010)

Dykes, Benjamin trans. and ed., *The Forty Chapters of al-Kindī* (Minneapolis, MN: The Cazimi Press, 2011)

Dykes, Benjamin trans. and ed., *The Search of the Heart* (Minneapolis, MN: The Cazimi Press, 2011)

Dykes, Benjamin, trans. and ed., *The Book of the Nine Judges* (Minneapolis, MN: The Cazimi Press, 2011)

Lilly, William, *Christian Astrology*, vols. I-II, ed. David R. Roell (Abingdon, MD: Astrology Center of America, 2004) *A classic text, but sometimes harder for beginners to understand.*

Māshā'allāh, *On Reception*, in Dykes, Benjamin trans. and ed., *Works of Sahl & Māshā'allāh* (Golden Valley, MN: The Cazimi Press, 2008)

Elections

*Bonatti, Guido, *Bonatti on Elections*, trans. and ed. Benjamin N. Dykes (Minneapolis, MN: The Cazimi Press, 2010)

Dykes, Benjamin, *Traditional Electional Astrology* (Minneapolis, MN: The Cazimi Press, 2012)

Sahl bin Bishr, *On Elections*, in Dykes, Benjamin trans. and ed., *Works of Sahl & Māshā'allāh* (Golden Valley, MN: The Cazimi Press, 2008)

Mundane and weather

Abū Ma'shar al-Balhi, *On Historical Astrology: The Book of Religions and Dynasties (On the Great Conjunctions)*, vols. I-II, eds. and trans. Keiji Yamamoto and Charles Burnett (Leiden: Brill, 2000)

*Bonatti, Guido, *Bonatti on Mundane Astrology*, trans. and ed. Benjamin N. Dykes (Minneapolis, MN: The Cazimi Press, 2010)

Dykes, Benjamin, *The Astrology of the World: Tradtional Mundane Astrology* (several volumes) (Minneapolis, MN: The Cazimi Press, 2012)

Māshā'allāh, *On the Roots of Revolutions, Chapter on the Rains in the Year, On the Revolutions of the Years of the World*, in Dykes, Benjamin trans. and ed., *Works of Sahl & Māshā'allāh* (Golden Valley, MN: The Cazimi Press, 2008)

Ptolemy, Claudius, *Tetrabiblos* vol. II, trans. F.E. Robbins (Cambridge, MA: Harvard University Press, 1998)

Websites of Interest

ARHAT: www.robhand.com

Benjamin Dykes: www.bendykes.com

Bernadette Brady: www.bernadettebrady.com

Chris Brennan: www.chrisbrennanastrologer.com

Christopher Warnock: www.renaissanceastrology.com

David Hermandez (Spanish): www.astrologiaholistica.com

Deb Houlding (Skyscript): www.skyscript.co.uk

Demetra George: www.demetra-george.com

Hellenistic Astrology: www.hellenisticastrology.com

John Frawley: www.johnfrawley.com

Lee Lehman: www.leelehman.com

Project Hindsight: www.projecthindsight.com

Robert Zoller: www.virginastrology.com

Sue Ward: www.sue-ward.co.uk

APPENDIX B: THE *ESSENTIAL MEDIEVAL ASTROLOGY* CYCLE

The *Essential Medieval Astrology* cycle is a projected series of books which will redefine the contours of traditional astrology. Comprised mainly of translations of works by Persian and Arabic-speaking medieval astrologers, it will cover all major areas of astrology, including philosophical treatments and magic. The cycle will be accompanied by compilations of introductory works and readings on the one hand, and independent monographs and encyclopedic works on the other (including late medieval and Renaissance works of the Latin West). These books are available at www.bendykes.com.

I. Introductions
- *Introductions to Astrology*: Abū Ma'shar's *Abbreviation of the Introduction*, al-Qabīsī's *The Introduction to Astrology* (2010)
- Abū Ma'shar, *Great Introduction to the Knowledge of the Judgments of the Stars* (2012-13)
- *Basic Readings in Traditional Astrology* (2012-13)

II. Nativities
- *Persian Nativities I*: Māshā'allāh's *The Book of Aristotle*, Abū 'Alī al-Khayyāt's *On the Judgments of Nativities* (2009)
- *Persian Nativities II*: 'Umar al-Tabarī's *Three Books on Nativities*, Abū Bakr's *On Nativities* (2010)
- *Persian Nativities III*: Abū Ma'shar's *On the Revolutions of Nativities* (2010)

III. Questions (Horary)
- Hermann of Carinthia, *The Search of the Heart* (2011)
- Al-Kindī, *The Forty Chapters* (2011)
- Various, *The Book of the Nine Judges* (2011)

IV. Elections
- *Traditional Electional Astrology*: Abū Ma'shar's *On Elections* and *Flowers of Elections*; other minor works (2012)

V. Mundane Astrology
- *Astrology of the World* (several volumes): Abū Ma'shar's *On the Revolutions of the Years of the World*, *Book of Religions and Dynasties*, and *Flowers*, Sahl bin Bishr's *Prophetic Sayings*; lesser works on prices and weather (2012)

VI. Other Works

- Bonatti, Guido, *The Book of Astronomy* (2007)
- *Works of Sahl & Masha'allah* (2008)
- *A Course in Traditional Astrology* (TBA)
- Al-Rijāl, *On the Judgments of the Stars* (TBA)
- *Astrological Magic* (TBA)
- *The Latin Hermes* (TBA)
- Firmicus Maternus, *Mathesis* (TBA)

APPENDIX C: ANSWERS TO EXERCISES

Chapter 8: Using Dignities

1. The Moon in Cancer, Mercury in Gemini, Venus in Taurus, Jupiter in Pisces.
2. Mars in Cancer.
3. The Sun in Taurus, Saturn in Pisces.
4. Honest, respectable, good natured, religious or spiritual children; a generally good life; maybe interested in Jupiterian things like law or finance.

Chapter 9: Houses

1. The first house, because she is in Gemini, the rising sign.
2. The fourth house, because he is in Virgo, the fourth sign.
3. The tenth house, because he is in Pisces, the tenth sign.
4. The fourth house, because he is in Virgo, the fourth sign. He is strongly stimulated, because he is in an angular quadrant division.
5. Middling, because he is in a middling quadrant division as measured from the IC.
6. Strong, because he is in an angular quadrant division as measured from the MC.

Chapter 10: Aspects and Aversions: Sight and Blindness

1. No, she regards Taurus by a square, and Libra by a sextile.
2. No, they are in aversion.
3. Aries.
4. Yes, just barely. Mercury's orb is 7° on either side of him. His exact sextile will land on 12° 52' Virgo, so the sextile's orb will reach to 19° 52' Virgo. Saturn's orb is 9° on either side, so the orb around his body will reach back to 19° 39'. Their orbs just barely overlap. But the sextile would be much more active if the orb of one planet actually touched the both of the other.
5. No. The Moon's orb is 12°. Her exact opposition will land on 3° 32' Virgo, so the orb of her opposition can only reach 15° 32', not enough to overlap with Saturn's orb.

Chapter 12: Two Rules for Interpreting Charts

1. The finances are connected to friendships. Maybe friends help the native out financially, or the native is able to count on unexpected good luck (the eleventh) to aid the finances.
2. The native's profession is connected to burdens and slavery, or maybe even small animals. Most likely, the native labors without a lot of recognition. This is because the natures of the tenth and sixth do not agree very well: the tenth means recognition, the sixth means labor and obscurity.
3. The native's sense of identity and purpose is connected to children or pleasures. For example, the native might devote her life, or at least be emotionally dependent upon, her children's lives.

GLOSSARY

This glossary is largely identical to the one in my *Introductions to Traditional Astrology* (*ITA*). After most definitions is a reference to sections of *ITA* for further reading. Don't get too overwhelmed by the number of terms here: many of them you already know from modern astrology or this book, and some are variations on the same traditional word due to different translation practices. Some of the words also belong to more advanced techniques.

- **Advancing**. When a planet is in an **angle** or succeedent. See III.3 and the Introduction §6.
- **Ages of man**. A division of a typical human life span into periods ruled by planets as **time lords**. See VII.3.
- **Agreeing signs**. Groups of signs which share some kind of harmonious quality. See I.9.5-6.
- *Alcochoden*. Latin transliteration for *Kadukḫudhāh*.
- **Alien** (Lat. *alienus*). See **Peregrine.**
- *Almuten*. A Latin transliteration for *mubtazz*: see **Victor.**
- **Angles, succeedents, cadents**. A division of houses into three groups which show how powerfully and directly a planet acts. The angles are the 1st, 10th, 7th and 4th houses; the succeedents are the 2nd, 11th, 8th and 5th; the cadents are the 12th, 9th, 6th and 3rd. But the exact regions in question will depend upon whether and how one uses **whole-sign** and **quadrant houses**, especially since traditional texts refer to an angle or pivot (Gr. *kentron*, Ar. *watad*) as either (1) equivalent to the whole-sign angles from the **Ascendant**, or (2) the degrees of the **Ascendant-Midheaven** axes themselves, or (3) quadrant houses as measured from the degrees of the axes. See I.12-13 and III.3-4, and the Introduction §6.
- **Antiscia** (sing. *antiscion*), "throwing shadows." Refers to a degree mirrored across an axis drawn from 0° Capricorn to 0° Cancer. For example, 10° Cancer has 20° Gemini as its antiscion. See I.9.2.
- **Apogee**. Typically, the furthest point a planet can be from the earth on the circle of the **deferent**. See II.0-1.
- **Applying, application**. When a planet is in a state of **connection**, moving so as to make the connection exact. Planets **assembled** together or in **aspect** by sign and not yet connected by the relevant degrees, are only "wanting" to be connected.

- **Arisings.** See **Ascensions**.
- **Ascendant.** Usually the entire rising sign, but often specified as the exact rising degree. In **quadrant houses**, a pace following the exact rising degree up to the cusp of the 2nd house.
- **Ascensions.** Degrees on the celestial equator, measured in terms of how many degrees pass the meridian as an entire sign or **bound** (or other spans of zodiacal degrees) passes across the horizon. They are often used in the predictive technique of ascensional times, as an approximation for **directions**. See Appendix E.
- **Aspect/regard.** One planet aspects or regards another if they are in signs which are configured to each other by a **sextile**, **square**, **trine**, or **opposition**. See III.6 and **Whole signs**. A connection by degrees or orbs is a much more intense of an aspect.
- **Assembly.** When two or more planets are in the same sign, and more intensely if within 15°. See III.5.
- **Aversion.** Being in the second, sixth, eighth, or twelfth sign from a place. For instance, a planet in Gemini is in the twelfth from, and therefore in aversion to, Cancer.
- ***Azamene.*** Equivalent to **Chronic illness.**
- **Bad ones.** See **Benefic/malefic.**
- **Barring.** When a planet blocks another planet from completing a **connection**, either through its own body or ray. See III.14.
- **Benefic/malefic.** A division of the planets into groups that cause or signify typically "good" things (Jupiter, Venus, usually the Sun and Moon) or "bad" things (Mars, Saturn). Mercury is considered variable. See V.9.
- **Benevolents.** See **Benefic/malefic.**
- **Besieging.** Equivalent to **Enclosure**.
- **Bicorporeal signs.** Equivalent to "common" signs. See **Quadruplicity.**
- **Bodyguarding.** Planetary relationships in which some planet protects another, used in determining social eminence and prosperity. See III.28.
- **Bounds.** Unequal divisions of the zodiac in each sign, each bound being ruled by one of the five non-**luminaries**. Sometimes called "terms," they are one of the five classical **dignities.** See VII.4.
- **Bright, smoky, empty, dark degrees**. Certain degrees of the zodiac said to affect how conspicuous or obscure the significations of planets or the Ascendant are. See VII.7.

- **Burned up** (sometimes, "combust"). Normally, when a planet is between about 1° and 7.5° away from the Sun. See II.9-10, and **In the heart.**
- **Burnt path** (Lat. *via combusta*). A span of degrees in Libra and Scorpio in which a planet (especially the Moon) is considered to be harmed or less able to effect its significations. Some astrologers identify it as between 15° Libra and 15° Scorpio; others between the exact degree of the **fall** of the Sun in 19° Libra and the exact degree of the fall of the Moon in 3° Scorpio. See IV.3.
- *Bust.* Certain hours measured from the New Moon, in which it is considered favorable or unfavorable to undertake an action or perform an **election**. See VIII.4.
- **Cardinal.** Equivalent to "movable" signs. See **Quadruplicity.**
- **Cazimi:** see **In the heart.**
- **Celestial equator.** The projection of earth's equator out into the universe, forming one of the three principal celestial coordinate systems.
- **Choleric.** See **Humor.**
- **Chronic illness (degrees of).** Degrees which are especially said to indicate chronic illness, due to their association with certain fixed stars. See VII.10.
- **Collection.** When two planets **aspecting** each other but not in an applying **connection**, each apply to a third planet. See III.12.
- **Combust.** See **Burned up.**
- **Commanding/obeying.** A division of the signs into those which command or obey each other (used sometimes in **synastry**). See I.9.
- **Common signs.** See **Quadruplicity.**
- **Configured.** To be in a whole-sign **aspect**, though not necessarily by degree.
- **Conjunction (of planets).** See **Assembly** and **Connection.**
- **Conjunction/prevention.** The position of the New (conjunction) or Full (prevention) Moon most immediately prior to a **nativity** or other chart. For the prevention, some astrologers use the degree of the Moon, others the degree of the luminary which was above the earth at the time of the prevention. See VIII.1.2.
- **Connection.** When a planet applies to another planet (by body in the same sign, or by ray in **aspecting** signs), within a particular number of degrees up to exactness. See III.7.
- **Convertible signs.** Equivalent to "movable" signs. See **Quadruplicity.**

- **Corruption**. See **Detriment**.
- **Crooked/straight**. A division of the signs into those which rise quickly and are more parallel to the horizon (crooked), and those which arise more slowly and closer to a right angle from the horizon (straight or direct). The signs from Capricorn to Gemini are crooked; those from Cancer to Sagittarius are straight.
- **Crossing over**. When a planet begins to **separate** from an exact **connection**. See III.7-8.
- **Cutting of light**. Three ways in which a **connection** is prevented: either by **obstruction** from the following sign, **escape** within the same sign, or by **barring**. See III.23.
- *Darījān*. An alternative **face** system attributed to the Indians. See VII.6.
- **Decan**. Equivalent to **face**.
- **Deferent**. The circle on which a planet's **epicycle** travels. See II.0-1.
- **Descension**. Equivalent to **fall**.
- **Detriment** (or Ar. "corruption," "unhealthiness," "harm."). More broadly (as "corruption"), it refers to any way in which a planet is harmed or its operation thwarted (such as by being **burned up**). But it also (as "harm") refers specifically to the sign opposite a planet's **domicile**. Libra is the detriment of Mars. See I.6 and I.8.
- **Dexter**. "Right": see **Right/left**.
- **Diameter**. Equivalent to **Opposition**.
- **Dignity** (Lat. "worthiness"; Ar. *ḥazz*, "good fortune, allotment"). Any of five ways of assigning rulership or responsibility to a planet (or sometimes, to a **Node**) over some portion of the zodiac. They are often listed in the following order: **domicile, exaltation, triplicity, bound, face/decan**. Each dignity has its own meaning and effect and use, and two of them have opposites: the opposite of domicile is **detriment**, the opposite of exaltation is **fall**. See I.3, I.4, I.6-7, VII.4 for the assignments; I.8 for some descriptive analogies; VIII.2.1 and VIII.2.2*f* for some predictive uses of domiciles and bounds.
- **Directions**. A predictive technique which is more precise than using **ascensions**, and defined by Ptolemy in terms of proportional semi-arcs. There is some confusion in how directing works, because of the difference between the astronomical method of directions and how astrologers look at charts. Astronomically, a point in the chart (the significator) is considered as stationary, and other planets and their **aspects** by degree (or even

the **bounds**) are sent forth (promittors) as though the heavens keep turning by **primary motion**, until they come to the significator. The degrees
between the significator and promittor are converted into years of life. But
when looking at the chart, it seems as though the significator is being
released counterclockwise in the order of signs, so that it **distributes**
through the bounds or comes to the bodies or aspects of promittors.
Direction by **ascensions** takes the latter perspective, though the result is
the same. Some later astrologers allow the distance between a significa-
tor/releaser and the promittor to be measured in either direction, yielding
"converse" directions in addition to the classical "direct" directions. See
VIII.2.2, Appendix E, and Gansten.

- **Disregard**. Equivalent to **Separation**.
- **Distribution**. The **direction** of a **releaser** (often the degree of the
  Ascendant) through the **bounds**. The bound **Lord** of the distribution is
  the "distributor," and any body or ray which the **releaser** encounters is the
  "**partner**." See VIII.2.2f, and *PN3*.
- **Distributor**. The bound **Lord** of a **directed releaser**. See **Distribution.**
- **Diurnal/nocturnal**. See **Sect.**
- **Domain**. A **sect** and **gender**-based planetary condition. See III.2.
- **Domicile**. One of the five **dignities**. A sign of the zodiac, insofar as it is
  owned or managed by one of the planets. For example, Aries is the domi-
  cile of Mars, and so Mars is its domicile **Lord**. See I.6.
- **Doryphory** (Gr. *doruphoria*). Equivalent to **Bodyguarding**.
- **Dragon**: see **Node**.
- **Dodecametorion**. Equivalent to **Twelfth-part**.
- *Duodecima*. Equivalent to **Twelfth-part**.
- *Dustūriyyah*. Equivalent to **Bodyguarding**.
- **Eastern/western**. A position relative to the Sun, in which a planet either
  rises before the Sun (eastern) or sets after him (western). Usually called
  "oriental" and "occidental." Different astrologers have different definitions
  for exactly what counts as being eastern or western. See II.10.
- **Ecliptic**. The path defined by the Sun's motion through the zodiac,
  defined as having 0° ecliptical latitude.
- **Election** (lit. "choice"). The deliberate choosing of an appropriate time to
  undertake an action, or determining when to avoid an action; but astrologers normally refer to the chart of the time itself as an election.

- **Element**. One of the four basic qualities. fire, air, water, earth) describing how matter and energy operate, and used to describe the significations and operations of planets and signs. They are usually described by pairs of four other basic qualities (hot, cold, wet, dry). For example, Aries is a fiery sign, and hot and dry; Mercury is typically treated as cold and dry (earthy). See I.3, I.7, and Book V.
- **Emptiness of the course.** Medievally, when a planet does not complete a **connection** for as long as it is in its current sign. In Hellenistic astrology, when a planet does not complete a connection within the next 30°. See III.9.
- **Enclosure.** When a planet has the rays or bodies of the **malefics** (or alternatively, the **benefics**) on either side of it, by degree or sign. See IV.4.2.
- **Epicycle.** A circle on the **deferent**, on which a planet turns. See II.0-1.
- **Equant.** A circle used to measure the average position of a planet. See II.0-1.
- **Escape.** When a planet wants to **connect** with a second one, but the second one moves into the next sign before it is completed, and the first planet makes a **connection** with a different, unrelated one instead. See III.22.
- **Essential/accidental.** A common way of distinguishing a planet's conditions, usually according to **dignity** (essential, I.2) and some other condition such as its **aspects** (accidental). See IV.1-5 for many accidental conditions.
- **Exaltation.** One of the five **dignities**. A sign in which a planet (or sometimes, a **Node**) signifies its matter in a particularly authoritative and refined way. The exaltation is sometimes identified with a particular degree in that sign. See I.6.
- **Face.** One of the five **dignities**. The zodiac is divided into 36 faces of 10° each, starting with the beginning of Aries. See I.5.
- **Facing.** A relationship between a planet and a **luminary**, if their respective signs are configured at the same distance as their **domiciles** are. For example, Leo (ruled by the Sun) is two signs to the **right** of Libra (ruled by Venus). When Venus is **western** and two signs away from wherever the Sun is, she will be in the facing of the Sun. See II.11.
- **Fall.** The sign opposite a planet's **exaltation**. See I.6.
- **Feminine.** See **Gender**.

- **Feral.** Equivalent to **Wildness.**
- *Firdārīyyah* (pl. *firdārīyyāt*). A **time lord** method in which planets rule different periods of life, with each period broken down into sub-periods. See VII.1.
- **Firm.** For firm signs, see **Quadruplicity.** For the houses, see **Angles.**
- **Fixed.** See **Quadruplicity.**
- **Foreign** (Lat. *extraneus*). Usually equivalent to **peregrine.**
- **Fortunes.** See **Benefic/malefic.**
- **Gender.** The division of signs, degrees, planets and hours into masculine and feminine groups. See I.3, V.10, V.14, VII.8.
- **Generosity and benefits.** Favorable relationships between signs and planets, as defined in III.26.
- **Good ones.** See **Benefic/malefic.**
- **Greater, middle, lesser years.** See **Planetary years.**
- **Ḥalb.** Probably Pahlavi for "sect," but normally describes a rejoicing condition: see III.2.
- **Ḥayyiz.** Arabic for "domain," normally a gender-intensified condition of *ḥalb.* See III.2.
- **Hexagon.** Equivalent to **Sextile.**
- *Hīlāj* (From the Pahlavi for "releaser"). Equivalent to **Releaser.**
- **Horary astrology.** The branch of astrology concerned with asking and answering questions.
- **Hours (planetary).** The assigning of rulership over hours of the day and night to planets. The hours of daylight (and night, respectively) are divided by 12, and each period is ruled first by the planet ruling that day, then the rest in descending planetary order. For example, on Sunday the Sun rules the first planetary "hour" from daybreak, then Venus, then Mercury, the Moon, Saturn, and so on. See V.13.
- **Humor.** Any one of four fluids in the body (according to traditional medicine), the balance between which determines one's health and **temperament** (outlook and energy level). Choler or yellow bile is associated with fire and the choleric temperament; blood is associated with air and the sanguine temperament; phlegm is associated with water and the phlegmatic temperament; black bile is associated with earth and the melancholic temperament. See I.3.
- **In the heart.** Often called *cazimi* in English texts, from the Ar. *kaṣmīmī.* A planet is in the heart of the Sun when it is either in the same degree as the

Sun (according to Sahl bin Bishr and Rhetorius), or within 16' of longitude from him. See II.9.

- **Indicator.** A degree which is supposed to indicate the approximate position of the degree of the natal **Ascendant**, in cases where the time of birth is uncertain. See VIII.1.2.
- **Inferior.** The planets lower than the Sun: Venus, Mercury, Moon.
- **Infortunes.** See **Benefic/malefic.**
- *'Ittiṣāl.* Equivalent to **connection.**
- **Joys.** Places in which the planets are said to "rejoice" in acting or signifying their natures. Joys by house are found in I.16; by sign in I.10.7.
- *Jārbakhtār* (From the Pahlavi for "distributor of time"). Equivalent to **Distributor;** see **Distribution.**
- *Kadukhudhāh* (From the Pahlavi for "domicile master"). One of the Lords of the longevity **releaser,** preferably the **bound Lord.** It is also equivalent to the **distributor** when directing any releaser through the bounds. See VIII.1.3.
- *Kaṣmīmī*: see **In the heart.**
- **Kingdom.** Equivalent to **exaltation.**
- **Largesse and recompense.** A reciprocal relation in which one planet is rescued from being in its own **fall** or a **well,** and then returns the favor when the other planet is in its fall or well. See III.24.
- **Leader** (Lat. *dux*). Equivalent to a **significator** for some topic. The Arabic word for "significator" means to indicate something by pointing the way toward something: thus the significator for a topic or matter "leads" the astrologer to some answer. Used by some less popular Latin translators (such as Hugo of Santalla and Hermann of Carinthia).
- **Lord of the Year.** The **domicile Lord** of a **profection.** The Sun and Moon are not allowed to be primary Lords of the Year, according to Persian doctrine. See VIII.2.1 and VIII.3.2, and Appendix F.
- **Lord.** A designation for the planet which has a particular **dignity,** but when used alone it usually means the **domicile** Lord. For example, Mars is the Lord of Aries.
- **Lot.** Sometimes called "Parts." A place (often treated as equivalent to an entire sign) expressing a ratio derived from the position of three other parts of a chart. Normally, the distance between two places is measured in zodiacal order from one to the other, and this distance is projected forward from some other place (usually the Ascendant): where the counting

stops, is the Lot. Lots are used both interpretively and predictively. See Book VI.

- **Luminary.** The Sun or Moon.
- **Malefic.** See **Benefic/malefic.**
- **Malevolents.** See **Benefic/malefic.**
- **Masculine.** See **Gender.**
- **Melancholic.** See **Humor.**
- **Midheaven.** Either the tenth sign from the **Ascendant,** or the zodiacal degree on which the celestial meridian falls.
- **Movable signs.** See **Quadruplicity.**
- *Mubtazz.* See **Victor.**
- **Mutable signs.** Equivalent to "common" signs. See **Quadruplicity.**
- *Namūdār.* Equivalent to **Indicator.**
- **Native.** The person whose birth chart it is.
- **Nativity.** Technically, a birth itself, but used by astrologers to describe the chart cast for the moment of a birth.
- **Ninth-parts.** Divisions of each sign into 9 equal parts of 3° 20' apiece, each ruled by a planet. Used predictively by some astrologers as part of the suite of **revolution** techniques. See VII.5.
- **Nobility.** Equivalent to **exaltation.**
- **Node.** The point on the ecliptic where a planet passes into northward latitude (its North Node or Head of the Dragon) or into southern latitude (its South Node or Tail of the Dragon). Normally only the Moon's Nodes are considered. See II.5 and V.8.
- **Northern/southern.** Either planets in northern or southern latitude in the zodiac (relative to the ecliptic), or in northern or southern declination relative to the celestial equator. See I.10.1.
- **Oblique ascensions.** The **ascensions** used in making predictions by ascensional times or primary **directions.**
- **Obstruction.** When one planet is moving towards a second (wanting to be **connected** to it), but a third one in a later degrees goes **retrograde,** connects with the second one, and then with the first one. See III.21.
- **Occidental.** See **Eastern/western.**
- **Opening of the portals/doors.** Times of likely weather changes and rain, determined by certain **transits.** See VIII.3.4.

- **Opposition.** An **aspect** either by **whole sign** or degree, in which the signs have a 180° relation to each other: for example, a planet in Aries is opposed to one in Libra.
- **Orbs/bodies.** Called "orb" by the Latins, and "body" (*jirm*) by Arabic astrologers. A space of power or influence on each side of a planet's body or position, used to determine the intensity of interaction between different planets. See II.6.
- **Oriental.** See **Eastern/western**.
- **Overcoming.** When a planet is in the eleventh, tenth, or ninth sign from another planet (i.e., in a superior **sextile, square,** or **trine aspect**), though being in the tenth sign is considered a more dominant or even domineering position. See IV.4.1 and *PN3*'s Introduction, §15.
- **Part.** See **Lot**.
- **Partner.** The body or ray of any planet which a **directed releaser** encounters while being **distributed** through the **bounds**.
- **Peregrine.** When a planet is not in one of its five **dignities**. See I.9.
- **Phlegmatic.** See **Humor**.
- **Pitted degrees.** Equivalent to **Welled degrees**.
- **Pivot.** Equivalent to **Angle**.
- **Planetary years.** Periods of years which the planets signify according to various conditions. See VII.2.
- **Prevention.** See **Conjunction/prevention**.
- **Primary directions.** See **Directions**.
- **Primary motion.** The clockwise or east-to-west motion of the heavens.
- **Profection** (Lat. *profectio*, "advancement, setting out"). A predictive technique in which some part of a chart (usually the **Ascendant**) is advanced either by an entire sign or in 30° increments for each year of life. See VIII.2.1 and VIII.3.2, and the sources in Appendix F.
- **Prohibition.** Equivalent to **Barring**.
- **Promittor** (lit., something "sent forward"). A point which is **directed** to a **significator**, or to which a significator is **released** or directed (depending on how one views the mechanics of directions).
- **Pushing.** What the planet making an applying **connection** does to the one **receiving** it. See III.15-18.
- ***Qasim/qismah***: Arabic terms for **distributor** and **distribution**.
- **Quadrant houses.** A division of the heavens into twelve spaces which overlap the **whole signs**, and are assigned to topics of life and ways of

measuring strength (such as Porphyry, Alchabitius Semi-Arc, or Regiomontanus houses). For example, if the Midheaven fell into the eleventh sign, the space between the Midheaven and the Ascendant would be divided into sections that overlap and are not coincident with the signs. See I.12 and the Introduction §6.

- **Quadruplicity.** A "fourfold" group of signs indicating certain shared patterns of behavior. The movable (or cardinal or convertible) signs are those through which new states of being are quickly formed (including the seasons): Aries, Cancer, Libra, Capricorn. The fixed (sometimes "firm") signs are those through which matters are fixed and lasting in their character: Taurus, Leo, Scorpio, Aquarius. The common (or mutable or bicorporeal) signs are those which make a transition and partake both of quick change and fixed qualities: Gemini, Virgo, Sagittarius, Pisces. See I.10.5.
- **Quaesited/quesited.** In **horary** astrology, the matter asked about.
- **Querent.** In **horary** astrology, the person asking the question (or the person on behalf of whom one asks).
- **Reception.** What a planet does when another planet **pushes** to it, but especially when they are related by **dignity** or by a **trine** or **sextile** from an **agreeing** sign of various types. See III.25.
- **Reflection.** When two planets are in **aversion** to each other, but a third planet either **collects** or **transfers** their light. If it collects, it reflects the light elsewhere. See III.13.
- **Refrenation.** See **Revoking.**
- **Regard.** Equivalent to **Aspect.**
- **Releaser.** The point which is the focus of a **direction**. In determining longevity, it is the one among a standard set of possible points which has certain qualifications (see VIII.1.3). In annual predictions one either directs or **distributes** the longevity releaser, or any one of a number of points for particular topics, or else the degree of the **Ascendant** as a default releaser. Many astrologers direct the degree of the Ascendant of the **revolution** chart itself as a releaser.
- **Remote.** Equivalent to **cadent**: see **Angle.**
- **Retreating.** When a planet is in a cadent place. See III.4 and the Introduction §6, and **Angle.**
- **Retrograde.** When a planet seems to move backwards or clockwise relative to the signs and fixed stars. See II.8 and II.10.

- **Return.** Equivalent to **Revolution**.
- **Returning.** What a **burned up** or **retrograde** planet does when another planet **pushes** to it. See III.19.
- **Revoking.** When a planet making an applying **connection** stations and turns **retrograde**, not completing the connection. See III.20.
- **Revolution.** Sometimes called the "cycle" or "transfer" or "change-over" of a year. Technically, the **transiting** position of planets and the **Ascendant** at the moment the Sun returns to a particular place in the zodiac: in the case of nativities, when he returns to his exact natal position; in mundane astrology, usually when he makes his ingress into 0° Aries. But the revolution is also understood to involve an entire suite of predictive techniques, including **distribution, profections,** and *firdārīyyāt.* See *PN3.*
- **Right ascensions.** Degrees on the celestial equator, particularly those which move across the meridian when calculating arcs for **ascensions** and **directions**.
- **Right/left.** Right (or "dexter") degrees and **aspects** are those earlier in the zodiac relative to a planet or sign, up to the **opposition**; left (or "sinister") degrees and aspects are those later in the zodiac. For example, if a planet is in Capricorn, its right aspects will be towards Scorpio, Libra, and Virgo; its left aspects will be towards Pisces, Aries, and Taurus. See III.6.
- **Root.** A chart used as a basis for another chart; a root particularly describes something considered to have concrete being of its own. For example, a **nativity** acts as a root for an **election**, so that when planning an election one must make it harmonize with the nativity.
- *Sālkhudhāy* (from Pahlavi, "Lord of the Year"). Equivalent to the **Lord of the Year**.
- **Sanguine.** See **Humor**.
- **Scorched.** See **Burned up.**
- **Secondary motion.** The counter-clockwise motion of planets forward in the zodiac.
- **Sect.** A division of charts, planets, and signs into "diurnal/day" and "nocturnal/night." Charts are diurnal if the Sun is above the horizon, else they are nocturnal. Planets are divided into sects as shown in V.11. Masculine signs (Aries, Gemini, *etc.*) are diurnal, the feminine signs (Taurus, Cancer, *etc.*) are nocturnal.

- **Seeing, hearing, listening signs**. A way of associating signs similar to **commanding/obeying**. See Paul of Alexandria's version in the two figures attached to I.9.6.
- **Separation**. When planets have completed a **connection** by **assembly** or **aspect**, and move away from one another. See III.8.
- **Sextile**. An **aspect** either by **whole sign** or degree, in which the signs have a 60° relation to each other: for example, Aries and Gemini.
- **Significator**. Either (1) a planet or point in a chart which indicates or signifies something for a topic (either through its own character, or house position, or rulerships, *etc*.), or (2) the point which is **released** in primary **directions**.
- **Sinister**. "Left": see **Right/left**.
- **Slavery**. Equivalent to **fall**.
- **Spearbearing**. Equivalent to **Bodyguarding**.
- **Square**. An **aspect** either by **whole sign** or degree, in which the signs have a 90° relation to each other: for example, Aries and Cancer.
- **Stake**. Equivalent to **Angle**.
- **Sublunar world**. The world of the four **elements** below the sphere of the Moon, in classical cosmology.
- **Succeedent**. See **Angle**.
- **Superior**. The planets higher than the Sun: Saturn, Jupiter, Mars.
- **Synastry**. The comparison of two or more charts to determine compatibility, usually in romantic relationships or friendships. See *BA* Appendix C for a discussion and references for friendship, and *BA* III.7.11 and III.12.7.
- *Tasyīr* (Ar. "dispatching, sending out"). Equivalent to primary **directions**.
- **Temperament**. The particular mixture (sometimes, "complexion") of **elements** or **humors** which determines a person's or planet's typical behavior, outlook, and energy level.
- **Tetragon**. Equivalent to **Square**.
- **Time lord**. A planet ruling over some period of time according to one of the classical predictive techniques. For example, the **Lord of the Year** is the time lord over a **profection**.
- **Transfer**. When one planet **separates** from one planet, and **connects** to another. See III.11.
- **Transit**. The passing of one planet across another planet or point (by body or **aspect** by exact degree), or through a particular sign (even in a **whole-**

sign relation to some point of interest). In traditional astrology, not every transit is significant; for example, transits of **time lords** or of planets in the **whole-sign angles** of a **profection** might be preferred to others. See VIII.2.4 and *PN3*.

- **Translation.** Equivalent to **Transfer.**
- **Trigon.** Equivalent to **Trine.**
- **Trine.** An **aspect** either by **whole sign** or degree, in which the signs have a 120° relation to each other: for example, Aries and Leo.
- **Turn** (Ar. *dawr*). A predictive term in which responsibilities for being a **time lord** rotates between different planets. See VIII.2.3 for one use of the turn.
- **Twelfth-parts.** Signs of the zodiac defined by 2.5° divisions of other signs. For example, the twelfth-part of 4° Gemini is Cancer. See IV.6.
- **Under rays.** When a planet is between approximately 7.5° and 15° from the Sun, and not visible either when rising before the Sun or setting after him. Some astrologers distinguish the distances for individual planets (which is more astronomically accurate). See II.10.
- *Via combusta.* See **Burnt path.**
- **Victor** (Ar. *mubtazz*). A planet identified as being the most authoritative either for a particular topic (I.18) or for a chart as a whole (VIII.1.4).
- **Void in course.** Equivalent to **Emptiness of the course.**
- **Well.** A degree in which a planet is said to be more obscure in its operation. See VII.9.
- **Western.** See **Eastern/western.**
- **Whole signs.** The oldest system of assigning house topics and **aspects**. The entire sign on the horizon (the **Ascendant**) is the first house, the entire second sign is the second house, and so on. Likewise, aspects are considered first of all according to signs: planets in Aries aspect or regard Gemini as a whole, even if aspects by exact degree are more intense. See I.12, III.6, and the Introduction §6.
- **Wildness.** When a planet is not **aspected** by any other planet, for as long as it is in its current sign. See III.10.

BIBLIOGRAPHY

Abū Ma'shar, *Abū Ma'shar on Historical Astrology: The Book of Religions and Dynasties*, trans. and ed. Keiji Yamamoto and Charles Burnett (Leiden: Brill, 2000)

Aristotle, *Physics*, trans. Robin Waterfield (Oxford: Oxford University Press, 1996)

Dykes, Benjamin trans. and ed., *Introductions to Traditional Astrology: Abū Ma'shar & al-Qabīsī* (Minneapolis, MN: The Cazimi Press, 2010)

Holden, James H., *A History of Horoscopic Astrology* (Tempe, AZ: American Federation of Astrologers, Inc., 2006)

Ibn Ezra, Abraham, *The Beginning of Wisdom*, trans. Meira Epstein, ed. Robert Hand (Arhat Publications, 1998)

Morin, Jean-Baptiste, *The Morinus System of Horoscope Interpretation (Astrologia Gallica* Book 21), trans. Richard S. Baldwin (Washington, DC: The American Federation of Astrologers, Inc., 1974)

Paulus Alexandrinus, *Late Classical Astrology: Paulus Alexandrinus and Olympiodorus*, trans. Dorian Gieseler Greenbaum, ed. Robert Hand (Reston, VA: ARHAT Publications, 2001)

Pingree, David, *From Astral Omens to Astrology: From Babylon to Bīkīner* (Rome: Istituto italiano per L'Africa e L'Oriente, 1997)

Sahl bin Bishr, *The Fifty Judgments*, in Dykes, Benjamin trans. and ed., *Works of Sahl & Māshā'allāh* (Golden Valley, MN: The Cazimi Press, 2008)

Valens, Vettius, *The Anthology*, vols. I-VII, ed. Robert Hand, trans. Robert Schmidt (Berkeley Springs, WV: The Golden Hind Press, 1993-2001)

CPSIA information can be obtained
at www.ICGtesting.com
Printed in the USA
FFOW02n1031040914
7137FF